THE
MILITARY FAMILY:

A CASUALTY OF WAR

As told by a former military spouse

JACQUELINE M. ARNOLD

PRESS

First Printing: November 2013

The Military Family: A Casualty of War
As Told By a Former Military Spouse
by Jacqueline M. Arnold

Printed in the United States of America

ISBN 9781498409902

www.xulonpress.com

DEDICATION

To my children: Kyle Stratton, Korey Morgan, Kaitlin Marie, Kerrigan Michael and Kellie Camille
For being brave soldiers

Acknowledgements

- *To all of our military friends who became like family. To the units where we served and the communities which welcomed us. To the commanders and their wives and the base support battalions and the staff who served. To all who became our family and our support when our own were miles and miles away.*

- *To Regina Smith who helped me bring my Korey Morgan into the world. To Regina and Kyle and Sam and Carinda and Richard and Susan and Chris and Christine and Bill and Mercedes and Bill and Diane and so many others who opened their hearts and their families to include ours. To Rosemary Griggs and so, so many more military families who sympathized with our family and the women at every post who loved our family and held us up.*

- *To my mother, Camille, who leaves a legacy of love in all she does. She is my best friend. She listened, she loved and she gave me encouragement when I needed it. She took my little ducks under her wing and loved them with me. She is the greatest mommy in the world. We have traveled and explored and persevered and believed together. She was very much a part of our military life.*

- *To each of my children. I'm so sorry that you had to live through the battles. I wish you each a life of peace and love with all my heart.*

- *To the 235th BSB and the 104th ASG and the peers who became my friends and life support.*

- *To my dear mentors Skip Walker and Pam Estes; I was privileged to know you, saddened to say goodbye. You taught me so very much about life and leadership. I hope you're dancing with the angels.*

- *To the German communities who opened their arms and their hearts and made life a fairytale dream. It was a privilege and an honor to be a Fasching Princezzen. Your hearts are warm and lovely. It was a dream come true travelling your beautiful country.*

- *To my family in Newport News, VA. Peach Orchard held some of my darkest days and my fondest memories. We were a community of family raising family, embracing America and making our young way. Thank you for those days.*

- *To my Wilshire family in Peachtree City, GA for sheltering us from the storm and helping us raise our family during a period of great transition.*

- *To Sylvia Arnold, bless you for being the mother of five boys (and a girl!). For raising soldiers who serve. And for praying so faithfully. God has a special place in heaven for you.*

- *And, of course, Ann McIndoo, my Author's Coach, who got this book out of my head and into my hands.*

TABLE OF CONTENTS

Introduction

War rages on the home front, as well as the battlefield. I would know, I am Jacqueline Arnold and I am a casualty of war, as is my family. I was a military spouse married to an Army aviator from Desert Storm through Operation Enduring Freedom. I signed up for twenty-three years of service as a military spouse, not knowing the hardships and sacrifices to be endured.

As a mother of five children, through multiple war campaigns and deployments, I know a thing or two about single parenting, stress, change, perseverance and courage. I know about sacrifice, hardship, chaos and uncertainty as well as the effects of war on a soldier and his family.

Through hopes and dreams and mandatory moves, career changes and unemployment, through childbearing and child rearing, I know the cost of freedom. I know *that my family and I became casualties of the war when after years of endurance, we lost the battle to a fractured family and finally to divorce. You will not find our name or our stories on any war memorial.*

I know what it is like to care for a sick child alone; to worry if your baby will ever meet his daddy, and to realize that the Grand Canyon of anger and pain may prevent him from ever getting to know any of his children, mostly growing up, wishing he was home.

I am here to tell a story, my story, of what it is like as a military spouse and how war affects our children and takes its toll on families. I am here to shed light on the sacrifices made by the entire family and to give a voice to the military spouses who often go unnoticed in the campaign and to grant an opportunity for awareness and an understanding from the community which is served.

For the children who are born into the military and all of its orders, rules and protocol and mostly, to create an understanding for every American so they may open their eyes to the military community.

And through my story, just perhaps, start an entire movement to celebrate our country anew and to foster a spirit of understanding and compassion extended to families left behind to wait during deployments, whose lives are forever on hold and whose hearts are forever seared.

I share my story in detail that each citizen may find the role in these continuous campaigns to reach out and support the military families left waiting, parenting alone in isolation and often, desperation. That with helping hands extended, the blanket of comfort and care can keep the family held together until the soldier returns to his home and his family from his military campaigns. Well loved, cared for and in-tact.

I dream of a day where the Spirit of America is revived and renewed. Let us shed light on the other casualties of war and the impact of the families and let us give America an opportunity to take action.

You see, after many deployments, after several rewarding campaigns, after many, many tours of duty, moves and transitions, after separations, pains, wounds and losses, after anger that builds up and bitterness that took root, my family fractured, was separated and impacted by the war campaigns which led to the demise of our family as a unit and my dream of being married forever with a family that was healthy, whole and in-tact.

I hope my family's sacrifice for the campaigns is inspirational, enlightening and unforgettable – enough to motivate you to reach out to others, to lend a helping hand and encourage military families and spouses currently enduring the separation and hardships of deployment, still. This is not a just any soldier's war, this is America's war. I challenge you to take a stand and get involved.

CHAPTER ONE

PRINCE CHARMING

Vince and Jackie,
Jackie and Vince
Two-gether in Love
Princess and Prince
-Vincent J. Arnold

Every girl dreams of being Cinderella and marrying a knight in shining armor, living in a grand home and living *happily ever after*. That's how my fairytale began. Prince charming was tall, dark, Italian and handsome. He was playful, lively and fun.

He stole my heart right from the start. He promised me the moon, exotic travel, a life of military protocol, formal balls and a passport. He shared my dream of having many kids; a lively Italian home. I was swept away. He was my prince; surely, we would live happily ever after together forever.

I didn't know that happily ever after would include five children, one delivered with his daddy at war, a number of moves, deployments and war campaigns too many to count, the collection of twenty three thousand pounds of household goods, sacrificing my own career dreams, bootstrap living, cinderblock quarters and never again returning to my home state or my family.

Again, I didn't know my vials of tears would accumulate to gallons or that my vow to stay married forever, my dream to celebrate a silver wedding anniversary and to give my children a loving, peaceful home, would be shattered by divorce and lingering memories of separations and hardship. All seven of us would be forever wounded and become a different kind of casualty of war. I didn't enlist, so I never expected to be so fully impacted by the mission, but I would soon discover the cost of enlisting.

When I met my husband, the allure of adventure and a life in the military sounded exotic and enticing. I thought that meant that I would travel a lot and I would entertain often. As an officer's wife, I knew that I would have a prominent place in the community and be able to use my skills of making new friends, volunteering, organizing group functions and serving off of silver platters with ease. I was delighted that this would be something I would be a part of.

I welcomed the opportunity to dress up in ball gowns and go to formal affairs. I welcomed the opportunity to see my man in uniform – especially his dress blues. When we first met, he was in the Coast Guard and those dress blues of the Coast Guard had a special appeal. When we first met, he had served about six years and had high hopes of becoming an aviator. The Coast Guard had an education restriction, so he would eventually have to pursue a career in the Army to pursue his dream of flying.

We teased that Coast Guard Blue was the Coast Guard Country Club. In the Coast Guard, enlistees stand duty about once a month. Coast Guardsmen go to work as if they were going to a nine to five job; they have a typical work day, only rather loosely structured. Typically, he would be home before I got off of work– done with his duty day at three thirty in the afternoon. His free schedule made it seem as if he didn't have a job, it was if he wasn't in the military. It was a great routine. But, it made it seem as if it was make believe – not a military position. There was no hardship in this role. He didn't seem like he had a duty, the way a soldier does. Though both are involved in the safety and security of our country, Coastguardsmen and Army soldiers fill two different roles and fulfill two different missions.

The Coast Guard wasn't a realistic picture of what was to come in the Army. The Army was a completely different operation. Over time, with global demands placed on the Army and its troops, it became even more unrealistic. Once war and deployments began and the new Army – today's Army – evolved, there was no similarity at all to the Coast Guard routine we were once familiar with.

Prior to our being married, while we were still engaged, I would get just a taste of what was to be our new way of life with our first unwelcomed separation. He had orders for a deployment to Thule, Greenland. Since we were still just engaged, I wasn't authorized to accompany him. Instead, I marked time by accepting a position that would further my own career and piqued my interest for travel and adventure. I moved from Alabama to Arkansas to manage a large apartment community, a sister company to the company which managed the complex where we met. It was similar to the position I had when we met but it was a promotion to a new property and a management position and would help me pass the time while he was away.

At the airport we said our goodbyes longingly, slowly; it was sad to say goodbye. Wrapped in his arms, he gave me a parting kiss that will linger with me always. In my heart, something had already changed – a sadness that recognized the unstoppable change on the horizon. I knew with this separation things would never be the same. We had had an amazing engagement period to get to know one another and fall in love and enjoy one another's constant companionship, the separation and loneliness would be a dagger to the heart.

We had so much fun together making life an adventure as we got to know each other dating and enjoying life around our work schedules and time flew by. Now we would have to put all of that behind us. There was no more freedom to enjoy one another, have control over our free time or determine our time together. Now, there was a greater authority ready to dictate when our hands could touch, when our eyes could meet, when our lives could play on. It was so sad that it was time for the deployment to begin already. Even though we had plenty of time to prepare emotionally, we still weren't ready to embrace the moment and accept the final goodbye. My heart wrenched. The tears spilled. He lingered to kiss me longer. It's funny how you have defining moments. In your heart of hearts, in the moment, you just know that this is the moment that will change your future. It was true for this moment.

We met on a rainy August day. I was an apartment manager and he was a resident in the popular apartment complex. I was prompted by a senior manager to "call one of the guys in apartment #1906" because one of them would be willing to pick up and haul supplies for the upcoming social. Vincent Arnold happened to be the one who picked up the phone when I called. He did agree to pick up and deliver and insisted I ride along for the task.

It was a rainy night and he was driving his brother's Jeep Wrangler for the pickup and delivery. I was feeling more than under the weather that night, but went along to do my job. On the way, he flirted and teased me about the boyfriend I had and he boldly claimed, "I'm going to steal you away. I'm going to marry you."

What a bold claim for someone who had just met me! Apparently, he had seen me in the property office on another occasion and tried to get my attention then, but I was rather dismissive, caught up in my work at the time.

After that rainy night, he did indeed steal me away. I left him a note in his mailbox.

About last night, you stole my heart.

He was charming and entertaining, fun and gregarious. He was Italian and good looking. How could I help myself? Within a few short weeks, he was already claiming, "I'm going to marry you" with a more serious tone. And I was sure of it, too. Eight months later he officially proposed. As sure as we were of our decision to be together, his sweaty palms gave indication to the reality of the commitment.

We were walking in the mall one day, hand in hand, his palms clammy and sweaty and I commented about them teasingly. We were walking through the J C Penney store and he suddenly spun around and got on one knee and choked a bit as he tried to spit out the words.

"Will you hang out with me for a long, long time?"

I laughed, stunned, uncertain of what was happening. "What?" was my shocked response.

He repeated the same question again. "Will you hang out with me for a long, long, long time?"

He had added a 'long' for emphasis on the second go 'round, but still no "Will you marry me words were heard."

"Well," I said demurely, "I'll have to sleep on that."

"Well if you have to think about it, I might change my mind," he said, equally stunned.

I laughed and embarrassed at my response, quickly said, "Well, yes, then."

He stood up and hugged me as I squealed and we stumbled over to the store entrance. I took a seat on the podium where the mannequins were perched at the main entrance of the store. We were both shaking as he slipped the marquis-shaped ring on my finger. We marveled at what had just transpired and were lost in time, forgetting about the store or the shoppers passing by. Eventually, we looked about and realized we should do something to celebrate. Within sight was a McDonald's and we went in and absentmindedly ordered a cheeseburger. Taking our order and our seat in a nearby booth, we reflected on all that had just happened.

It was five short months later that he would transition from the Coast Guard to the Army to become a pilot and be sent to Thule, Greenland for his first deployment and our first separation as a young couple. This was the moment we were facing now at the airport as we said our goodbyes. It was a heartfelt goodbye and we were ignorant of the many, many times yet to come where we would say goodbye so he could serve the country.

Not yet married, I soon took that promotion and flew to Little Rock to manage the apartments, but I would soon realize how family and a community of friends would be critical to enduring long separations and deployments in the future and son grew lonely in Arkansas.

When he returned from Greenland, the thought of me staying put in Arkansas was not rational. The miles were many and besides, the promises made to incent me to move with my company were verbal and not honored by the new administration, so it was an easy decision to move back South where we could have a greater chance of being together.

So when he returned from the deployment, he jumped in the car and headed to Arkansas to pack my belongings and bring me back to the south where he would soon start Helicopter Aviation Flight School and I would temporarily live with my mother in South Florida, separated from him still.

Within weeks, I gave up any thoughts of my own career, attachment to my mother and my family and moved just outside the military post's gate to follow my soldier as would be the norm and the expectation going forward. This would be one of many moves I would make for his military career. And the back and forth, together apart, temporary housing, quick change of plans would also become a normal routine for us as we launched and followed his military career with the U. S. Army.

CHAPTER TWO

A FAIRY TALE WEDDING FROM FLIGHT SCHOOL

E xotic travel, living overseas, parties to attend, social affairs and formal balls – it all seems like a fairy tale. But, there's a cost to being associated with the military and dressing up as a fairy princess. There's a cost for all of the benefits you receive. Remember, the famous motto? The Army didn't issue the soldier a spouse, so don't expect them to recognize that spouse. (The Army has since come a long way in recognizing spouses as family members and has spent a great deal of time and money creating programs and resources to support the military spouse and family. Many of these programs and resources were not available to us during our years of service). While I discovered the community of people to be very supportive and generous to the spouses, there just isn't a place for them in the mission. The needs, dreams and priorities of the spouse and family don't really fit; they just try to fit in where they can, letting go of their highest priorities and hope for the best.

When the soldier is in flight school, he has no rights– just many responsibilities. The beginning of flight school is the most stringent time of expectation, structure and discipline. It's called, Warrant Officer Candidate School; WOC D, for short. The Army is trying to rewire the person's independent thinking, for which they brought them on, rewiring them so they are stripped of self and only think when told to do so. There is no freedom here and very limited tolerance for family and significant others. Instead of a family unit, soldiers are being immersed into the Army unit.

Flight school is in the heart of Army Aviation Headquarters at Fort Rucker, Alabama. It's in the South, but still so far away from where I was in South Florida. The miles separated us; my heart was breaking every day. When he would finally call – sometimes three, four or five days in between, my voice would immediately shake, relieved he hadn't forgotten me. It was so hard to wait for the time to pass to hear from him. Life came to a standstill in between and I had opportunity to doubt and wonder how our lives would change with this new military.

I would often wonder how much longer I would have to wait to hear from him the next time.

From his perspective, his days were filled with constant stress, labor and taskings. He was constantly under pressure to improve his performance and when he failed, he was given an opportunity to think about it by having to walk paces in the barracks quad. It was agonizing for him. The extra duty would eliminate any opportunity he might have had to call me. Calls were very limited during that initial phase. I just hung on hoping he would be able to call and that he would.

After a month or two of this, I decided to move in with another candidate's wife; a total stranger, just to be near him. This candidate's wife had a home just outside the gates. I don't even remember how we met, just the common bond of suffering; having someone we loved stuck on the other side of the gates while we waited it out for their release and success. By moving in with her, we had each other for support, comfort and distraction. I also helped her care for her two young children. She was warm and welcoming and like most military families who are connected by this special bond, we soon became fast friends. It was a good thing because we would soon spend our days living in close quarters in her two bedroom house. It was something I would become accustomed to in the military – making lasting friendships with strangers.

Military families become your family away from home. She offered me refuge and just a few miles outside the gate, I could know that I was close to him as I slept at night.

There is another cost to falling in love with a soldier and choosing to spend your life supporting his mission and the military's course. I had recently graduated with my degree in journalism and was ready to position myself for a progressive career in journalism. I hoped to work for newspapers and go into publishing, perhaps working for a magazine in a high-rise, maybe in the middle of New York City. I was always struck by the big city lights, having come from Miami, Florida; I thought it would be exciting to work in a big city with a fast pace. But there is a cost when you are a military spouse and I was soon to be one so I had to learn at an early stage, that every dream and hope you have, will likely be compromised or placed on hold for an indefinite period of time. Whatever wish you have, the Army will have a mission to undermine it. It's just the way things come to pass. You spend a career trying to surrender to this. And you want to surrender to it. My heart is with my country and my soldier and our service to the

Army, but it becomes a painful calling and many things are sacrificed along the way.

As I traveled to the small town of Daleville, Alabama, just outside the gates of Fort Rucker, I realized there wouldn't be a ton of opportunity for launching my career or big city lights or a corner office with a majestic view of the big city – we're talking rural Alabama here. I would have to start small, so I started knocking on doors and I ended up as a reporter at a local weekly newspaper.

This brought me further from my career aspirations of publishing in a high rise, but closer to the military post and my soldier who held my heart. The proximity made me feel as if I were still part of his life even if being 'locked up' in WOC D meant only seeing one another for two hours on Wednesday and the short visiting period on family visitation day on the weekend. Even if it meant barely being able to sit next to one another without a critical eye of a commanding chaperone, I looked forward to the time we could be together.

Visitations were structured. There was ongoing oversight; we were never without chaperones. In fact, holding hands was of limits, but we often snuck our hands to overlap. Kissing was taboo. I was so thrilled to be close to him, to see his engaging smile, to have him speak to me face to face and reassure me we were right for each other and the waiting was worth it.

During visitations we would mingle with the other candidates and their wives and girls, too. It was a good time to make new friends. Mostly there were other spouses, girlfriends were the minority. It was good to connect with others who were experiencing the same angst over the mandatory separation.

Flight school was a dream of his I wanted to support. I knew there would be a cost. I also knew about dreams. I might have had dreams of a publishing or writing career, but before that, I also had stars in my eyes to be a star on Broadway. I had applied for the American Academy of Dramatic Arts through a very special audition-only process.

I minored in theatre in college, had many leading roles through high school and college, including a lot of awards for stage and theatre. I had a passion for performing and I knew I could make a career out of it. I had to drive to Sarasota, Florida for the audition. I was ecstatic to know that I had been accepted based on my performance and application. But, it wouldn't be a dream I could follow. My husband's acceptance to flight school would be the choice. I quickly realized that I would be making a choice early on. A theatre gig wouldn't fit very well with change of duty stations, families and deployments. My heart and the feelings in my heart were much stronger than any stage lights or any calling to be on Broadway. God would redeem that with a leading actress win in community theatre down the road, anyway.

The newspaper job was a good fit for my writing skills and mixing with the community, but I wasn't very good at the dirty details of small town reporting. For instance, when there was a car accident, I was sent to chase the car and the ambulance to find out the details. I was new to this kind of assignment. I was trying to be respectful of the victims so I stood on the other side of the street to get a photo and somebody came up to me and said, "You know, if you are the reporter, you need to get into the details of it and move closer." I was so embarrassed, but they were right. I would have to learn to intrude on the privacy of others to get the real story into print. That was difficult to get in the middle of.

I had to learn to grow and get out of my comfort zone. In fact, another one of the stories I covered was a helicopter crash. I had to traipse through the woods to find the crash debris, climb over logs and take close up pictures of this horrid scene; a scene that could very potentially have been my soon to be husband. It was in my face and raw and real but I was called to do my job and think like a journalist–not the glamour of the high rise and publishing job I had hoped for.

In flight school, he was learning to fly helicopters. He flew in very small helicopters before transitioning to larger helicopters. He went from tiny Scouts to the Hueys and any time he flew I knew there was risk involved. But I also knew that was his dream and his passion and I wanted to support him and encourage him and pretend there was no risk at all; just a day at work. From the sidelines at the Fort Rucker Army airfield I watched him take his solo flight and with my breath held and my heart thumping in my chest, I stood in the field so he could see me present and I applauded him, denying any trace of fear.

I knew there would be a cost for this life, and sacrifices, but I had no clue as to how high the cost that would tax our relationship or the dreams we had. For my part, I tried to be a great encourager. We became the social coordinator of his 'Purple Flight'. Flight colors identified each unit and his was known as 'Purple Flight'. I encouraged him to throw our name in the ring as social coordinators so we would get to know each of the couples in the unit and so we would have instant friends. By leading and being 'Out Front,' he would know I supported his career decision and he would have greater opportunities to be seen as a leader.

As the Purple Flight coordinator he had to give the graduation speech at the commencement exercises for his unit which also stretched him. I thought it was a perfect fit and a great start to what I envisioned the military would be like–leadership, events, fundraising and fun; this role was out of his comfort zone, but a good decision nonetheless. My vision of military life was not exactly as I envisioned and eventually rained on my wedding day bliss.

We were engaged in April and chose an April wedding for the following year, but our excitement and impatience was waning and my mother insisted we change our Jacksonville, Fl wedding plans to Fort Lauderdale, Fl–our home town–this is only fair to the mother-of-the-bride, she insisted. Our wedding was planned for the spring, with the intent that he would have been graduated from flight school at the time. With the change, it upset the dates and so we had to adjust by accelerating the day of our wedding to the month of January. Instead of our beautiful spring wedding of April, we would have it in winter in order to fit it in the calendar and around his flight school schedule. We had to consider flight training and his anticipated date for his solo flight. We were eager to be together, making it easier to agree to the change.

January was a very cold month, but in South Florida, everything is sunny year-round, so the date change was to our benefit. The military command was not as agreeable to the change. In fact, when the military heard the news of the wedding, the command was less than pleased and tried to get us to change the date yet again.

We are both from big Italian traditional Catholic families and we had dreams of a large wedding. In fact, my Cinderella dream was to have a wedding in a large down town cathedral which was already reserved for the original April date in Jacksonville, FL. The wedding move from Jacksonville to Fort Lauderdale made it no longer possible to marry in a cathedral because the Catholic Church had rules that you had to be an active member of the parish in order to have a wedding in a cathedral. Stationed miles away, that wasn't possible. I gave up that dream as we planned our wedding in the new location and settled on a simple church with family history.

We planned a beautiful wedding, in spite of the limitations and the rescheduling. It was going to be a large sit down affair with lots and lots of people, a formal event where everyone would dress to the nines. It couldn't be held in a cathedral, but I could still have a fabulous reception and the wedding of my little girl dreams.

First the mother of the bride, now the Army had other thoughts about our wedding. Since he was still in the initial part of WOC D flight school, he had to petition the commander for permission to marry, to even take on a wife, let alone have the ceremony in the middle of that particular phase of flight school. Additionally, he had to ask for permission to leave the state for the weekend in order that we might celebrate our wedding with our family in South Florida.

The Army doesn't typically allow time off for flight school – at all, so after three hundred invitations were already in the mail and time approached to the wedding day, they agreed that he could get married, but he could only have twenty-four hours leave for the ceremony.

We had to again petition the unit, "Can we please have more time?" Reluctantly, they agreed that we could have forty eight hours. How disheartening. I had waited a lifetime to be a bride and I had less than 48 hours to enjoy my moment. There was pressure for him too. In less than three days' time, from Friday through Sunday, he had to catch a flight, fly to Fort Lauderdale where he met me, host our family and his with a meal for our dress rehearsal and partake in all of the celebrations and festivities that are traditional to a wedding. The next day, with very limited fanfare, we prepared for our wedding.

In spite of the limitations, our evening wedding was beautiful. We had many symbolic moments and events that made it memorable. We lit the traditional candle, we had traditional music, our parents, our family and friends were present, we passed Italian wedding cookies and dance all night. We were married in the church where my brother was married and where a nephew had been baptized; so it wasn't the cathedral, but it was still meaningful to our family.

It would eventually become the church that our children would become baptized in. Since we were stationed other places, we would travel home to use this church for baptism sacraments so our family could share in our joy. A beautiful wedding, a special day, but there were signs already at the wedding that would make one scratch their head. We released two live doves of peace and yet, one bird would not fly away. My sister, the maid of honor, thought it would be funny to capture the bird and leave it in our honeymoon suite later that night, as we had discovered when we arrived; it cooed all night.

There were also other little glitches; my sister was giving us the gift of the honeymoon suite. When we arrived, we learned they didn't have a reservation for the honeymoon suite at all and due to the filming of Caddy Shack II that weekend, the property was quite full; so instead of the honeymoon suite, they gave us the handicapped suite.

Odd symbols of what would happen to our marriage as we limped along, month to month, year to year. In spite of the Army trying to hold us back by not allowing much time, we got married in South Florida that weekend.

The day was beautiful and the wedding met every expectation of my childhood dreams. It was truly one of the most fun nights of my life. When we woke up, so very tired on Sunday morning following the wedding, we very quickly opened our wedding presents, perched on the edge of the living room floor and left them in Florida for shipping later, got on a plane and flew back to flight school where we kissed goodbye at the gate and he went to be sequestered, or what they call 'locked up', for another six weeks.

I returned alone to our new apartment to unpack, settle in and wish for my bridegroom to move home soon. The six weeks that were to be our honeymoon became six weeks of anguish as we were forced to be separated as he finished a portion of his flight training. I was permitted to visit him for two hours on Wednesday evening and two hours on Saturday morning where we could sit on the lawn to catch up and even as newlyweds, steal a brush of the hand. Not as much as hand holding was permitted in public, but we always tried to sneak when commanders weren't watching. As young newlyweds should want to be, we yearned to be close to one another, but the flight school schedule didn't allow for that.

Just in the way a little girl dreams of having a spectacular wedding with luncheons and festivities and a fabulous honeymoon in an exotic location, I secretly yearned for that also. I mourned the loss of not getting to know my new spouse in a fun location, where time stood still and we could just spend time with one another. But that was not meant to be for us. He would make it up in other ways as we traveled to exotic locations during duty stations yet to come. But, it was never the same.

I later discovered that even the Bible says nothing should separate a man and a woman during the first year of marriage. Not events or responsibilities, for in the first year you are to get to know one another and build your relationship on a strong foundation.

> *If a man has recently married, he must not be sent to war or have any other duty laid on him. For one year he is to be free to stay at home and bring happiness to the wife he has married.* -Deuteronomy 24:5

Wish someone would have counseled us on that then. It was a missed opportunity that would deeply impact our beginnings. I held it in and from time to time, it caused some dissatisfaction; it's something that is buried deeper in my heart than I understood and it is something, even though it wasn't intentional, that I could never seem to release. Likely, it was just one more sacrifice in the bucket of sacrifices that I didn't embrace.

I understood that I was marrying him at flight school; I understood that the Army would have a hold on him. But when we were engaged, he was in the Coast Guard; when we were married, he transitioned to the Army. Two different organizations, cultures and philosophies; I had no understanding of the impact it would have on our family, on our relationship or how I would respond to that. Truth is, he didn't either. Not that either of us had experience with the Army, but the Army was a changing Army about the time we signed up and the demands would only increase with time.

Truly, one does not really know what the military is like until they are full enlisted, fully signed up and then, there is no turning back. Once you are in the Army, you are in to stay. A career soldier just bellies up, sucks it up and soldiers on. An Army's wife just puts on her pretty Polly face and cries behind closed doors, thrusting her stiff upper lift upward as farewells are exchanged and marking the days of separation off the calendar. That's not to say, military wives are milk toast. We are courageous and brave and understand and support the mission and our spouse's devotion to service, but anyone who says there is no sacrifice or pain or resistance, isn't being honest. Life is endured because the hardships are real.

CHAPTER THREE

AN ARMY OF WIVES

My exposure to women in the military community came early. I had to rely on strangers to open up their homes and give me a place to stay from the very beginning of my arrival at Fort Rucker. Every day, in between the days I visited my then fiancé, soon to be spouse, I spent many hours of time with these girls, getting to know them, who they were and what their dreams and hopes were for their marriage, for their husband's military careers and their families.

We spent time when we were together to go to church, we had lunch together, we met once a week to encourage and support one another; they were becoming my community of family. We dreamed of where the Army would take us and if we'd stay together for future duty stations.

Encountering community in the military is like no other; we were all in the same boat of hope and happenstance.

Your family is thousands of miles away, your siblings are thousands of miles away, you have no best friends yet and there is no one you know with any history or understanding of who you are. Your heart is sad because you are separated from the one you love. You have to lean on someone; you can't just isolate yourself into a puddle of self-pity and women who share a similar story easily become your friends.

You get to know them quickly and soon jump into the friendship and soon they become your sisters; they become the women you can count on in the middle of the night when your husband is off at war. They become the women who become the aunts to your children; they become the women who fill the void of your empty heart. They are the ones you call when fear is overwhelming or pain stabs at your heart. They nurse maid you when you are sick and console you when you are sad and you do the same for them and often. They become the friends who form a sisterhood of support.

Somehow we endured that time of separation during flight school when we were first married. I busied myself with work from independent home party sales to catering for small events to substitute teaching and soon there was more freedom of time for us to see one another. As he advanced, we might have a chance to spend time together on a Saturday hosting a fundraiser for the unit, like when we hosted a car wash. Other times, the wives just socialized with one another looking for ways to be purposeful in our day and feel connected to our spouses when visitation was limited. There was the occasional social for new officer's wives and I often brought an appetizer to share. My cooking became great time filler and soon I was catering for events and even compiled a cookbook, hoping to use it as a fundraiser for the unit.

Eventually, about two months after we were married, he was released from the lock up phase and he moved home into our first apartment just outside the gates. It was the type of apartment memories are made in. You know the one, where the 3 X 3 magazine stand doubles as your dining table and the apartment has no dish-washer, but to impress the bride, the groom agrees to do all the dishes for the lifetime of the apartment residence, where the day bed was our sofa in the living room and the overflow of belongings filled the tiny second bed-room, leaving it unusable. We were off to a typical start and yet so blessed, not having to live on base and finally together as a couple.

We celebrated our six month anniversary with a big dinner at home. I greeted him at the door after work in my wedding dress, table set and candles lit only to discover June is the sixth month of the year, but not the sixth month anniversary of our January wedding! We laughed at ourselves and moved into our true sixth month anniversary the very next month in a different way. Though when we were discussing wedding and family plans we mutually agreed to wait about three years to think about adding a family, by six months we had both changed our minds. By the end of September, instead of me in a wedding dress and a romantic dinner, he came home to jars of baby food on the table.

With our baby news also came the end of his flight school training and news of our first tour of duty. I was hoping to go overseas early on in our career, so the children could be raised near my family and their cousins, planning a state side tour of duty later in his career, but not so fast. Our first duty station would be stateside, to Fort Campbell, Kentucky. It's funny how I just never considered that I could live in Kentucky. I was a Florida girl with travel dreams, how did Kentucky fit into those dreams; a beautiful state, but not very far from my southern comfort.

The duty post was spread over the boundary lines of two states, the unit address in Kentucky and our home address was to be in Clarksville, Tennessee. When we arrived at Fort Campbell, Ky, our first official duty station, we discovered there were no available quarters on post and the apartment complexes had waiting lists so we were left to look at buying a home. I was delighted, but he was more than a little on edge with fear and the burden to provide.

We arrived at the housing community office to check in and found it was already full. While the Army called us to this station, they didn't guarantee available housing. We toured the base from enlisted to officer's quarters and I remember feeling so sad for the state of enlisted housing. What a shame, these families were making such great sacrifices and the state of the living quarters was near condemned. Maybe it was my first time impression, but I remember the quarters being very close together, not well kempt, dirty, a few screens awry and marked up, worn out front doors. It was a sad welcome. As a warrant officer, we would have been given different quarters anyway, maybe even a two bedroom cinderblock house, with a baby on the way. It still didn't hold much appeal. With no availability anyway, we chose to look for an apartment nearby. To our disappointment, the nearby apartments were full too.

There was no place to live. We were required to be there for his first tour of duty and no place to lay our heads; not showing up for duty was not an option. It could have been a time of panic, after all we had little pocket money let alone money for a down payment on a house in a location we would be only temporarily. But the real estate signs just outside the gate promoted VA loans with no money down and only $500 closing costs to move in. It made it easier to consider the possibility of buying a home.

Not that there were many homes to even be purchased–I recall having about three to choose from. Luckily one was a brand new home. I was thrilled to have a home to nest in, a home to buy furniture for, a home to paint, a home to dream in and a home to bring babies home to in. I saw our dreams unfolding, not dollar signs.

My husband knew the reality of a military paycheck and was nervous about the enormous responsibility. He knew his military paycheck as a Warrant Officer wouldn't be enough to stretch a mortgage and provide for a new baby, so we had to be careful with our decision. Purchasing that home made him sweat bullets. I believe it was the beginning of his anxiety induced from the pressure of taking care of his family, which he so desired to do, and balancing the demands of his Army career and the transitory nature of his commitment.

He knew that he had to be at the duty station and it made logical sense we needed a place to stay and without available housing, there were no other options, but boy was that hard to reconcile. The VA loan made it a little easier for him to swallow as did the supply and demand which we contended would help resale when the inevitable time to move duty stations would again arrive. We purchased the house against his natural instincts, but it was the first crack in the solid foundation and the beginning of our family's financial stress.

We walked into what would become our home and I fell in love right away. There were three bedrooms; perfect for what I was hoping would be room for a growing family. There was a beautiful kitchen where I could cook Italian meals and a nice, big yard where my husband would find himself on Saturdays mowing the lawn.

I knew that it would be a good home for us. It had many great features, a large garage with a workshop bench where he could tinker; lots of counters for cooking and baking in the kitchen, a home where we could start our family. I was a naïve Army wife unaware that buying a home didn't mean putting down roots; it was still a temporary residence until the next set of orders. We wouldn't be there for very long, it was part of our Army story. You are never anywhere long; for some families six months and for other families eighteen months.

We managed a three year tour paid at a price of several field deployments and one war campaign to *Desert Storm*. And, as military careers go, we were very lucky – Fort Rucker, Fort Campbell, Fulda, Germany, Ansbach,

Germany, Newport News, VA, Fort Bragg, NC and a retirement move to Florida and eventually Peachtree City, GA. It was the separations that were more numerous than the change of duty stations.

We had a beautiful home, he had a career, we had a child on the way, but our resources were very tight and we still had limited furniture in our new home. My papasan chair from college and the two wicker fan-back chairs from my first apartment became our living room furniture. This was rather difficult for my protruding pregnant belly to fit and in my desire to settle in. Furniture seemed like a reasonable request. To my pregnant self, it made logical sense, but it was much more than my husband was willing to extend on our limited income from the Army. We spent many hours negotiating the need for furniture. Eventually I discovered a fabulous living room set on clearance, including lamps, tables and couches- seven pieces in all, for less than six hundred dollars. Our job and our duty station might be temporary, but my life wasn't and I was ready to start furnishing our home; this seemed a reasonable thing to request.

I immediately had him sit on the couch and I showed off every piece as if I were the furniture salesperson. I thought it was such a value package, but when I told him the price, his face went ash white. He knew it was a reasonable purchase to make – like the house we purchased when we were without quarters, but the furniture was another burden both financially and emotionally. Furniture becomes a burden when it's time to change duty stations. The less you commit to at each duty station, the fewer obstacles there are to interfere with the mission.

In the Army, the more you acquire, the more you have to move and the more you move, the more stress it creates having to address all your belongings and prepare them for the move. The Army does move things when it's time to change duty stations but the more stuff, the more stress plain and simple.

Plus there is a weight limit, based on your rank, which is assessed on moving day. This was something I was reluctant to learn. I had an emotional attachment to things having lost many people close to me. And I love symbolism and often collected things when we travelled and with the birth of each child came additional gear and toys. I was trying to create a legacy in our home, establish our family and acquire heirlooms and treasures, but what I was creating was a burden.

The Army is more of a vagabond life and when you live station to station, hauling 15,000 – 20,000 pounds of household goods in your sack, it's not so easy. I never did get that lesson. I just hung on to the premise, life is short – we couldn't keep waiting to enjoy our lives and sometimes this meant acquiring new things. Plus, my premise was that you never know how long you might be at a station; this held true as we were extended in Germany and in Virginia, so simply get things when you determined you needed or wanted them not based on 'what if we move tomorrow.' For us, a family of eventually seven, that led to a lot of household baggage in more ways than one.

Before we even knew we would be heading to Germany and collecting so many treasures along the way, Fort Campbell, home of the 2/17th Cavalry, became our home base and where would find our closest community of family. As a newlywed, the Army of wives were especially welcoming to me. I soon saw how they would pull together for me in times of our first deployment; they would be there for me when I was in labor with my spouse off at war and when I was sick and couldn't care for myself or my children. So much change was on the horizon for a young military wife, it was awesome to have an Army of wives help me through the transition as I adjusted to this new life. I met the warmest and welcoming community of friends there. It was one of my cherished tours of duty and I loved the families, women and couples we would meet during this tour.

At the first meeting of the wives' group, I came to learn about each one of the unit wives and listened to the chatter from those more experienced than me with the ways of the Army, tours and deployments. There were different perspectives, those who had careers, some married to colonels, some married to majors, some new to the military, some who had been a part of the military for years and this was to be their family's life's work; their husband's chosen career. I met some that were moms, some that were countries away from their home and some that were excited to be their husband's right arm and best supporter. They were from different walks of life, but one common thread. And it was obvious they all had common threads in their hearts, as well. They loved their mates. The military was a love-hate-angst relationship, but they were proud of the role they had and the part they played to support their soldier, their country and the mission.

At my first wives' support group meeting, they were talking away as we prepared for our soldier's first separation and field training assignment in the unit. We were preparing for JRTC field training for a three week field deployment, where the husbands go for training to hone their skills and to be prepared for war movements and quick response actions. It is staged in Arkansas where terrain is better suited and heavy equipment is already in place for practice. The wives, of course, would keep the home fires burning while the soldiers trained. The meeting was to give us information regarding the training and available support services to help us stay afloat during their departure.

We were at this wives' meeting talking about how it would feel with our husbands gone, how our days would be structured, what it would look like, where would we spend our time, how we could connect with the community, how we could volunteer in our different areas of interest, how we could continue working on our careers and raising our children, for those who had children and so forth. I held several different positions during this duty station as a newspaper writer, editor and eventually as a substitute teacher . It was the women's roster I sometimes had to turn to at 9 pm the night before work to cover child care as the babies needed care. During this first deployment, I wasn't yet working since we were new to our station. I would have to find ways to fill my days.

While waiting for the meeting to start, the conversation was lively and I remember the chatter. One more experienced wife was talking to a younger wife saying, "Oh, I can't wait until the next deployment! How soon is that? Not soon enough!" Other women chuckled and chimed in, "Not soon enough! It has been too long;

it's time for a deployment – it's time for them to be on their way!"

I remember in the silence of my heart thinking, *I'll never be one of those wives; I'll never be like them. I will never want my spouse to go away on a deployment. He is too dear to me. I want to soak up every moment of him; I want to be near him every chance I get. I don't want him to deploy, I don't want to be separated.*

Little did I know that this upcoming field exercise was the beginning of many, many separations.

And that these separations would change our relationship and put tiny little holes in our hearts. Little did I know that separations, wars and deployments would come with increasing rapid fire and bring on stress, hardship, loss and sadness and would start to harden our hearts and create such tension that we would also be among those who sometimes looked forward to a few weeks of separation as times of peace; that in our separation we could retreat and lick our wounds, regroup and determine to begin again. I never looked forward to the longer deployments; I looked to those with dread and angst and sadness.

For this first separation, I looked for opportunities to connect with the military community. There are volunteer opportunities and many activities sponsored by the morale welfare and recreation facilities to support the family members of the soldiers who are on active duty or deployed so there are lots of things to choose from. There are so many ways to get involved; raising funds for the flights, for the next event or thinking of some charitable opportunity for the community or supporting another wife in one of their volunteer endeavors are popular options. There are things to do for recreation like go to the movies on post or explore outdoor recreation or head to the bowling alley; plenty of options on base.

I was always hosting an event. Often times I would volunteer to bake the cake for one of our ladies' events. Many times I would make the appetizers. I loved being a part of something bigger than me and contributing to a special event was so much fun. Our gatherings were a nice way to welcome new officer's wives with fanfare, with flowers, with homemade baked goods and soon this lead me to collect many recipes and format them into a cook book; I had help from the newspaper staff. Instead of doing car washes, which we had done plenty of, I thought the wives' group could benefit from some of the proceeds of the cookbook. In the end, it was another lost project; a great idea that didn't take flight. I invested the upfront money for the cost of the books, hoping the group would sell the books and I would recoup my costs. Everyone encouraged me in my idea and support of the fundraiser and I pursued the project, assembling and publishing it, but once it was time to kick off the sales campaign, they weren't as enthusiastic, realizing that they were only getting part of the proceeds from the book sales, but I had to recoup my investment; they weren't thrilled with that. There was no written guideline for this. This got tricky for the unit commanders. I ended up with cases of cookbooks.

Mostly I filled my time with the fellowship of new friends. Friendships were especially important in the military because the wives understood each other – we were all going through similar experiences. Many had experienced multiple separations, deployments and trainings and had plenty of first-hand experiences to share. They knew the stages of deployment before, during and after. The reactions and emotions are pretty typical and there was always someone who could give an encouraging word. Not many had been through a real war campaign and together we would experience that, figuring it out together as we went.

They became the family members that a working mom needed when she was raising children solo. I was soon writing for the community newspapers juggling as a newspaper editor and in need of a temporary 'aunt' or an alternate caregiver. Sometimes it would be late at night when I would find out I would need childcare the next morning. The Army community offered day care, but I wanted a personal touch. I relied on Army wives who were childcare providers in their homes, but sometimes their husbands were deployed in the middle of the night and it would upset their family and they needed time to regroup leaving them unable to meet my childcare needs the next work day.

At the last minute I would find myself in need of child care and all I would need to do was go through my unit roster and would surely find another wife willing to step forward and watch my children on short notice. They became my support group and it was an integral part of every tour we were on. It enabled me to keep working with confidence.

Deployments were a constant, but they weren't always scheduled until the last minute. There's a lot of equipment to schedule and human resource to move so the date isn't always easily pinned down. A deployment is when your husband is sent away for duty, sometimes to an unknown destination, for an unknown period of time. Your husband packs his Army-issued uniforms in a duffle bag, slings his bag over his shoulder and heads out the door for another long work assignment and you, the military wife, begin to mark off the days of separation on a calendar.

He packs his duty gear, often in the middle of the night and he boards an airplane to a destination you don't know even know of without first getting out a map and finding it. He prepares himself to carry out his mission in another region, sometimes in another time zone.

As a family, you hope they're infrequent, but with increased global activity the deployments happened closer and closer together straining our relationship and our hearts with increasing frequency. When we first joined the Army, deployments weren't even part of the career plan. Then the world landscape changed and it became a new Army, the way The Army was rapidly responding to meet the needs of a changing world. Deployments often meant that units and men had to be called to duty and activated on quick response. Consequently, families had to be emotionally prepared for the challenges and the goodbyes at any given time. Soldiers were always 'on the ready,' with this new mission and frequency of deployments. I was left to be both mother and father when he was deployed, soon it became a natural rhythm and his comings and goings were pretty seamless; I simply managed nearly all tasks at home and for the kids, so when he was gone, there was little disruption.

We chalked up countless deployments and separations, but I well remember him called to field duty for our first wedding anniversary, Desert Storm during my grandmother's funeral and the birth of our second child,

JRTC during my grandfather's funeral, Cyprus when I was expecting our fourth child and working full time, and Operation Enduring Freedom, when I was home with five, including one in need of specialty care and managing one through constant reflux. I can't remember the back to back deployments, the training missions, the nights of duty specifically, I only know there were so many family events missed, moments endured and extra burdens because our soldier was serving. I know I was experiencing early labor and he was at JRTC and then there was the year of Desert Storm – the farewell and the waiting. That was an incredulous year. Nine and a half months of deployment while pregnant and raising a strong-willed toddler, and the year my grandmother passed the week I was to deliver baby two. I was in early labor for a few weeks while he was on the front lines in Iraq, then my grandmother died, then he came home from war to a seven week old he didn't know, my father died four months later, my grandfather one month later; he was at JRTC for three weeks then so attending the funeral wasn't an option for me, and my uncle two months later, just before we packed up and headed out of country to our new assignment in Germany – he would fly ahead without us for two months; a lot of pain in one short year and a soldier far away. It was the sacrifice to be made. He was either preparing for a deployment and we were counting down until departure, involved in a deployment and we were counting down the days until he returned, or transitioning off of a deployment and we were counting down the days until life would soon be normal again. There are few calendar days where life is normal and settled. Peace is temporary. Change is the constant.

Everything in the military is temporary. Housing is temporary, where you are going to live sometimes in temporary quarters until your name moves down a list for available housing that will be more permanent – well, for your temporary tour of duty. Your unit could be temporary as you are reassigned to another one to make up for a shortage of personnel. You have to constantly make new friends and learn new commands. Change becomes the constant.

You learn to do this as part of the landscape. You can't take your time to slowly get to meet people because you are going to need that support group in a hurry as your soldier might be leaving for action or standing overnight duty soon and there will inevitably be a crisis just as you arrive. It's nice to have a support group to reach out to.

When you're expecting your first child and no family around, it's more than just nice; it's the thing that gives you courage to determine to make it work with a stiff

upper lip at first and then eventually you become a sea-
soned military wife and adjust, but your military family
is always a source of constant strength and encouragement. It takes a strong soldier to be a military wife, in
so many ways, it takes an Army of wives to support the
mission.

CHAPTER FOUR

PREGNANT AND CASUALTIES OF WAR

The more deployments, the more babies is the Army joke. And with more babies, more stuff is the reality. Babies, babies, babies. Oh, the joy of motherhood. Soon we would have not one or two, but five children. Pregnancy, a time of joy for young mothers and a time when you would think everything would be happy and joyful, but for a military wife, it can be a time of burden and often, going it alone, sifting through the sadness and the longing to share the excitement and trials of the pregnancy with the baby's father. We would be expecting the arrival of another baby, planning the nursery together–or at least, he would be there to listen while I bounced off decorating ideas and for the first, at least, we attended Lamaze classes together and if not at every false labor pain, he was present in the delivery room for our first son and fairly good odds, for four out of the five arrivals.

The military doesn't make adjustments or consider whether the wife is pregnant or not when it's time to go off to war, or for deployments or other military training. But, they surely had an impact on me as a mother, something I didn't anticipate when we were first married. Our first three children, especially, were deeply impacted by the military, deployments, moves, transitions and stress. Kyle, Korey and Kaitlin have experienced the active part duty service more so than the final two, who had the experience of retirement.

Kyle Stratton was our first child and son. In October as we were finishing up all the responsibilities of flight school and waiting on our first duty assignment and with it an impending move, we were excited to learn we would soon be expecting our first child. He was due in May and not before we would say goodbye to Fort Rucker and welcome Fort Campbell, Ky and the 2/17th Cavalry as our new home. As the time got closer to his deliver, I had early Braxton Hicks on and off and his daddy was deployed to NRTC training in another state. It was my first pregnancy, my family lived states away and I just wanted him to be near; it was our first baby together, after all.

I was nervous, I was excited and I was anticipating the baby we were to bring into the world and I wanted his daddy to be close so we could share the pains, my frustrations and anxieties, the little joys and have him to ask questions to: What was that bump? Help me hear the heartbeat. Is everything okay?

It would have been so nice to have his daddy near to hold his hand and help me through. I was fortunate enough to have the sympathy of the colonel's wife. She was kind to me and felt sympathy for me and our predicament the Army imposed. She wanted my husband to be near as well. It was about three weeks before my delivery date and every little contraction caused her to get nervous.

She called her husband and said, "Henry, I think Mrs. Arnold's husband needs to come home because she is going to have this baby any minute, I just know it!" My belly was protruding and contractions would come and go, but I still had a few weeks. All the excitement of the on and off contractions, did bring him home early by about a week, but not the baby. We showed up to the hospital and they sent us home and assured us that when it was truly time for the baby to come, we would definitely know.

As it turned out, Kyle Stratton arrived three days after his due date, and that month long of anticipation was just an anxious mommy on her first baby delivery. I was still grateful for his early return and the time we had to cherish the last days before baby arrived. Kyle's pregnancy was nothing compared to baby number two. Korey Morgan was due February the third. He would be stubborn as it turns out, and not arrive until February the sixteenth, but not before sending a lot of calamity and excitement ahead of time.

This was during the first war campaign, Desert Storm. In May, just after Kyle's first birthday, we found out we were going to be having a second child in February. It was August 2 when things heated up in the Middle East and about August 19th my husband would depart for Saudi Arabia for the Desert Storm war campaign. How could a young, pregnant wife possibly prepare emotionally for what lay ahead?

How could she help him say goodbye to their first child; her fifteen month old, who was confused and wanted his daddy to stay near? It tore at my heart that goodbye. I will never forget the moments as we said our goodbyes, looking at the child before me and feeling the child within my womb, and wondering if he would ever meet his daddy. The weeks passed slowly as my baby belly grew, I could see his elbow skirt across my belly and the protrusion of the skin on my belly; those shared moments of pregnancy would be missed, never recovered.

I thought that he would never get to know his daddy as the war developed and seemed to increase in intensity. We would follow it on the news; inviting it into our living rooms was as if we were right there, constantly on our mind. My mother came to keep us company through the last term of my pregnancy, helped with Kyle and kept watch on the news with me. I busied myself by sewing all of my maternity clothes and the nursery items for the baby's expected arrival. Often it was just a mask to conceal the torment of my emotions, wondering if his daddy would ever come home safely and be there in time for the delivery. Waiting for the baby was one thing – there would be a joyful ending – waiting on the campaign to end was another – not know how it would carry out or when it would end or what the outcome would be. Would I be able to ensure the safety and care of this little life until his father did return? It was an enormous weight I carried, praying that they would meet and I would have fulfilled my mission as a good Mother.

I had such a peaceful and easy first pregnancy and delivery that I didn't anticipate going into pre-term labor with my second child, but the stress of the war had a big impact on me; as well as the stress of being a single parent to the one child at home, a very strong-willed boy, who kept his mama's hands very full. I went into pre-term labor in early January. I knew better than to burden my husband with one more thing, so I kept it from him and my best friend helped me through it.

I didn't put any information about my pain in the letters I would send to him and on the rare occasion of his phone calls, I would never mention that I was in pre-term labor, that I was on medication to stay the labor or that there was anything wrong. Though I longed to share and was seconds away from bursting into tears, I would just tell him that everything was perfectly fine and the baby would come just in time for his return home; that of course, I knew he would be there for the baby's delivery. I always said not being there when a baby was born was a deal breaker and here I was about to eat my words. I reasoned a war was something he didn't really have control over and I would have to let that one go.

I said if there was a deal breaker that would be it. The daddy had to be home during the birth of his baby, right? Nothing could get in the way of that. However, war had its own agenda and he would not be home for the arrival of baby number two.

When that pre-term labor came on, I was scared. I called my best friend whose husband was deployed with mine, to bring me to the hospital. I was overwhelmed and I was afraid. I was afraid my baby would be born early and his lungs wouldn't be fully developed. I was afraid that my body couldn't handle this and the stress of my husband being gone, my family being hundreds of miles away, me being in the hospital and my now eighteen month old at home weighed heavily on my heart and my shoulders. I just wanted their daddy to come home. I wanted this pain to end.

I wanted at least to share with him that I was in the hospital. I wanted him to know what I was going through, what 'we' were experiencing, but I knew that the demands of war were greater and there was a price to pay for our freedom. I knew that he was in the right place, but it still made a woman lonely. It still made a girl yearn for her husband; for the father of the baby I was yet to hold in my hands. I needed something to hold on to.

The time of pregnancy should be a time that you are decorating nurseries, a time that you are anticipating the arrival of your baby – in joyful anticipation. It should be a time you are sharing with your spouse: what will the name be? What will he look like? Maybe it's a she, maybe it's a he? We don't even know yet!

I truly believe that if God wanted you to know whether you were having a boy or a girl that he would have allowed your baby belly to turn pink or blue, so I always wanted to wait in anticipation and allow the arrival of the baby and the surprise of the gender of the baby at birth.

I was in the hospital and the nurses were administering medicine–I hate to take medicine. Let alone, while I was pregnant. What effect would it have on the child I carried? No, I did not want to take this medicine. I was being obstinate but I knew I must, so I took the medicine to keep delivery at bay and the baby longer in my belly so his little the lungs could grow stronger, so this child would have every opportunity at good health and a good life and so this child would have the opportunity to meet its daddy.

I worried every day that something would happen, whether to the baby or me, or worse yet, his daddy. I felt so vulnerable and very fragile, but I knew I had to be strong for I had another child at home and I had a husband who was deployed at war, waiting to meet his child. Neither of us could have seen this coming when we were determined to be together and dreamed of starting a family.

The medicine they gave me, whatever it was called, was horrible. It made my skin crawl; it made me want to climb the walls. I did not know if I could bear to be on it for twelve hours, for eighteen hours, let alone, for seven days.

How would I manage this? If only my husband was here to calm me down, to reassure me, to help me have strength and focus on knowing I would make it through, but it wasn't to be. He was fighting away flies, working in an unairconditioned aircraft and sleeping on the sand, under the cover of his helicopter rotors. We were both fighting a war, so to speak, but he was fighting the war in Desert Storm and I was simply battling the test of time and emotions.

Luckily, I had the sweet goodness of Regina who had helped me through this time. It was her strength that got me through the medicine. She would be there with me every step of the way; she would become the pseudo dad in this relationship. Not exactly as I had planned, but this would become our normal: a military wife with a husband deployed overseas. We balanced each other while she raised her son and waited for her husband to come back, as well. We had plans one night in late January to have dinner together. I was going to bring my son Kyle over and we were just going to hang out and pretend life was normal. Almost overnight the war seemed to be picking up heat and fire. It was on all of the new channels everywhere we turned.

In fact, it was only a few days earlier that my babysitter's husband had been called away during the middle of the night to go serve overseas and we didn't know where he was going. It was part of the challenges of their family. He was Special Forces; she couldn't even know what country he was going to or what he was going to wrestle with. Too much information was a safety risk; too much information could put the family at home at risk as well as the military mission.

That was already weighing heavily on our minds as the news increased with stories of turbulence overseas. We were fearful that the action was picking up heat and that our husband's units were involved. It is one thing to know they are over there, but another to be aware they are involved in actual heated engagements. I had intentions of going over to her house for dinner. News flashed across the screen, a big banner sliding information across the television screen and a newscaster reporting that ground war had broken out that night. The ground war was in full action and full swing and sent fear and confusion racing through me and the wives' group.

What did that mean? I had never experienced a war before, I had known that my daddy fought in a war and I had heard his stories. I had known that many other much older friends had served at war and I had heard their stories. But that was a part of history, something I read in the history books. This couldn't possibly be happening in today's modern world – not in my world, to me and these babies of ours. This couldn't be a ground war of today that our U.S. troops were involved in; this couldn't be real. This had to be part of a history book. But, the television news confirmed it as a reality and the telephone chain had been activated in the wives group, making denial impossible. I called my friend and tried to beg out of dinner, "I couldn't possibly come to dinner with all this turmoil; let's cancel our plans."

But she was persistent, "Please come, it will be good for us. We'll stick together, we'll encourage one another. It's not good to be watching all this alone." And she was right. I knew it. Fear would take over and that wasn't good for the baby I was still carrying, trying to remain calm so that the pre-term labor didn't return.

I gathered my son, his toys and belongings and headed to her house for dinner. As I turned the handle of the front door to walk in, I cracked the door open and could see her and one or two other military wives standing around. I quickly closed the door and stepped back. I was fighting back tears and anxiety.

Immediately, I thought, *No, something terrible has happened. They're all gathered; I can't possibly walk in. I am feeling so weak; so overwhelmed. I just want him to be here, to hold me, to tell me he's coming home from all this chaos. I want him to be here to feel his baby in my belly. I don't want to experience this whole overwhelming thing on my own.*

But I knew I had to. They were waiting, whoever it was that was inside waiting. I took a deep breath and I opened the door. And, instead of sad news, there was happy news for just a brief moment. And then, instead of it being truly happy, it was sad.

The wives of all the soldiers who were in the midst of that current, heated battle, had gathered – these women who had become my family, to welcome the baby I carried, to give me a surprise baby shower and bring some joy to our day. Who could have known that the ground war would break out as we gathered for my baby shower?

God must have known. He knew that we needed each other. He knew that we needed a diversion. He knew that the baby I carried needed joy, that the mother who carried him needed joy in her spirit so that he could be joyful when he arrived. He planned the date of my baby shower. I was grateful for this gathering but it was so bittersweet.

After hugs and the astonished looks of surprise, within moments of my entering my friend's house, we were all glued to the television where news was just breaking of the war that had broken out; where the coverage continued, the moments escalated, where there was fear in the room, where our hearts tried to be still, where we looked for glimpses of our husbands on the screen and where the news casters reported the war, what would soon be history, that was taking place before our eyes.

We were also torn because we were trying to make light of the news both to deny the reality that our husbands and our country was in imminent danger and also for me, for this baby, for the friend who tried to honor me with a beautiful baby shower. We peeled ourselves away from the television as we cut the cake, as we tried to take in moments of discussion about the baby and tried to remember the moments of joy from my previous pregnancy and from each of the women gathered in their pregnancies; we were trying to have a baby shower.

We did our best that night to ignore the fact that my husband wasn't present and might not be for the birth or life of this baby we celebrated and that each of our husbands were at risk this night. We tried to ignore the reality of what our soldiers were experiencing. And in my heart, I comforted myself. I prayed. I begged God that he would allow this baby's father to come home, that he might meet his son; that I might not be a single mother for long.

The shower, however, was more like a shotgun wedding. No one lingered. It was over in but a brief hour or so, as I recall. We all quickly said our goodbyes, anxious to get back to cocoon in our own homes and the comforts of our beds where our husbands once slept.

I lay there that night and I rubbed my belly, trying to reassure both baby and momma. I snuggled next to my toddler son and dreamt about the moment their daddy would be returned safely to us. I took on a bigger burden that night. As I asked God to please allow me to carry this child to term, and that He would stay my pre-term labor and allow me the gift of a healthy baby and that He might bring his daddy home, that me might meet his father and that his father might know his son; that all would be healthy and well, and life would have hope of being restored to normal one day.

Two weeks later, my grandmother died on my due date. My husband was at war and I couldn't go to her funeral. And ten days later, Korey Morgan showed up in the world past his due date, with Regina as my birthing coach, big brawling shoulders and raven dark hair.

Pregnancy and labor in the military is definitely not part of the mission plan. You know, the military doesn't issue the soldier a wife, they certainly don't say to go out and have babies. We were definitely privileged to have regular pre-natal care and a guaranteed bed for delivery on base, but it wasn't always the most pleasant experience in the military. One moment in labor with this second child the midwife took her position and said, "It's time for the baby."

I cried out in pain and resistance, "His daddy isn't here to hold my hand or calm me down!", as most husbands are and I was looking for a little emotional salve in this final stage and she said, "Be quiet. It's going to hurt–just push!" That was a wake up moment. It wasn't exactly the bedside care you get in birthing rooms at civilian hospitals. Wow. Tough it up, like a good soldier's wife. The military care was top notch, it just didn't come with white kid gloves, so to speak. Again, a great benefit, but at a cost.

For example, I can remember having to make my own bed the day after delivery. I had just had my son the night before and the charge nurse came in and said, "Here are your sheets; change your bed." I didn't expect that; that wasn't exactly tales of the spa and labor suites my friends had had babies. Their stories always seemed to include lots of fresh flowers, balloons, surprise visitors and a constant stream of family and visitors bringing gifts and treats to greet the new baby and congratulate momma like a pampered princess. Not so much when the first order of business was changing my sheets or for my third daughter, getting up in the middle of the night to weigh the baby, precisely according to hospital regulations,

No pampering for Army wives who have to soldier up at home without the rucksack, but with a household to maintain and a family who often needs extra care. In six short weeks, I was in pre-term labor, had my surprise baby shower, war broke out, my grandmother died and my son was born. It was a very chaotic time and indicative of the year ahead.

We had news on television, but not many details of the unit's activities. No news was good news. But no new left your mind to wander and make things up. The quietness left your heart aching, but not daring to ask. We had no contact during this time and so very little prior to the events that erupted. There were no cell phones at that time (maybe for a commander's wife), land line usage was very limited, not very reliable and was delayed speaking. On the few times he was able to call, I was so happy to hear his voice but we ended up tripping over one another and we cut our calls short because it was so uncomfortable deciding whose turn it was to talk. There were a lot of awkward moments: who would speak first? What would we say next? What would we reveal about our realities? What will we conceal?

There was much of that going on both of our sides, so intimacy in our relationship was impacted. He certainly could not tell me about the realities of war, about sleeping in the sand under helicopter rotor blades on the edge of enemy lines. He couldn't tell me that there were bullets passing through the tent at night. He couldn't tell me that he was breaking out in sweats during the night wondering if he would ever make it home to see his children or longing for me and being next to me as he slept. It was best just to brush passed these thoughts and just focus on the few moments of connection.

He would tell me that he kept a family photo in his helmet. He kept one on his dash in the helicopter; a picture of his son, and me and him. This is what kept him going every day, he said. This is what motivated him to get through the stress and the chaos. This is what he held onto as his hope to return to his home. I waited for the surprise of his voice on those few and far between calls, even if not effective in communication, they were something to encourage me through the forced separation,

And at my home front, I picked up after a strong-willed child and counted down the days on the calendar. I would lock the door, but my son would find a way to rock on the rocking chair back and forth, back and forth, and time it perfectly to coincide with the swing of the screen door I had installed to keep him in the house when I might not be in the same room as him. He would time the rocker and the swing of the door to grab the handle and skirt out the front yard. He was always looking for a way for freedom and to be outside.

I would come back from folding a load of laundry and I would be looking around, *where was he?* Oh my word–out in the front yard, once again. He was spirited, he was strong-willed and he would never want to go to sleep at night so I was around the clock mommy with no daddy for relief. He would want me to stay up and read to him all night. I would surely love his daddy to be able to tuck him in and see how beautiful he was and how much he had grown. Every night we sang songs and prayed for Daddy's safety and to hurry home.

I was exhausted every morning with a growing baby, demands of a toddler and trying to find ways to keep myself distracted from the truth that my husband was gone overseas, deployed at war.

I spent hours on the baby's nursery, painting his room, sewing the layette for his nursery and creating ways to welcome him, following the traditions we had created with our first child.

In spite of all hope, his Daddy wouldn't be in the labor and delivery room, after all. The needs of the country trumped this delivery. It would be the coldest day of the year that he would decide to come. My mother came from Florida to help me but admitted she couldn't bear to see her own baby in pain as I went through delivery. It was great to have her as the grandmother I needed at home to take care of my first born as I turned to the task of delivering my second child.

On the coldest day of the year, my mother was at home with our first son and I was laboring at my best friend's home; she had become like an older sister to me; this stranger who had two of her own children showed up to help at one of the most important times in my life. Military wives are like that, they serve, they love, they help, and they just pick up and fill in where it's needed. Sooner or later, we all end up in that moment of need while our spouse is deployed.

Since we met at the beginning of our tour of duty at Fort Campbell, her first child was best pals with my first child and they entertained themselves for long hours of the day in the sandbox as we chatted in the kitchen, making a nice meal. We would create a family unit with our two sons and each other until our husbands came back for their seats at the table.

That night, I labored in her bed instead of laboring in mine with my husband next to my side. I labored on the couch with my eighteen month old climbing over my belly and her eighteen month old playing war next to me. Seventeen hours in all. After about twelve hours on the couch with the boys playing on me as a battle-field, I climbed into her bed and I rested, but not for long as I was immediately ignited by a very sharp pain that I had never experienced before; a lightning white streaked through my belly that told me it was time to go to the hospital, time for the baby to be born. Off to the hospital we went as my mother cared for our two boys.

The deployment stirred up so many questions since my husband was not there.

Who would be in the birthing room with me? Regina was a solid rock. She helped me through my breathing and my Lamaze so I could have a natural childbirth with my midwife. She wanted to film the birth for my husband. No, that would not work for me. She wanted to take pictures; I was uncomfortable enough, I wanted to focus on the delivery. I didn't want mementos of the delivery I just wanted him there. I wanted him there holding my hand, looking into my eyes, telling me I could make it through the next labor pain. The pains were very intense and rapid fire. He was difficult to deliver, but he came very quickly and I was grateful for that. In less than fifty six minutes, my eight pound, ten ounce boy, Korey Morgan was born. What a joy to hold him, to know that he was born healthy, to know that my friend was there helping me through and I didn't have to do this alone. In the military hospital that was very cold and sterile, it became colder still as I recognized a void created by this baby's daddy absence. This baby's daddy did not even know he had a child. Some things in life just don't seem fair. But a world at war is not fair, either. I held that little Humpty Dumpty of a baby with a big round face and big brown eyes and big strapping shoulders and tears streamed down as I looked into the eyes of our new son.

The war raged on and there would be no communications overseas at the time of his birth. It would be seven more days before his daddy even knew that he had a baby son. I wondered every day, *does his daddy know today? Did someone pass on the message?* The Red Cross helped get a message overseas.

It made it to the front lines on the third day, but it would be day seven when his daddy would read it and realize, with joyful tears, that his son had been born, his wife was healthy and he would have something to look forward to even, upon his return. That news, he said, would bring him hope through the war.

We both needed hope. When on February the third, my much loved grandmother, Caroline Demori would die and I couldn't go to the hospital or the funeral in New York City because it was my due date and my husband was deployed. It would be very sad to me to know that she would pass and I couldn't go to see where she was; I couldn't go to say goodbye in the hospital or at her grave site. I was feeling pretty bound and hopeless.

There were many summers I spent with her in New York for a week at a time, where I would grow close with my cousins and we would be taken downtown. And I would get to fall in love with Manhattan and Broadway, and all that New York City had to offer.

My grandmother would look forward to receiving me from the subway after a day of fun. She would have a meal cooked, my grandfather would be playing on his mandolin at night and we would chat in the rocking chairs. We would have fruits of their labor from the garden they had in the backyard, and they would tell me about my Italian heritage. She would tell me about my daddy, and we would grow close as grandmother and granddaughter. But I couldn't be there when she passed. It was very sad to me.

That was February third, and on February thirteenth, I anticipated the birth of my son and still he did not arrive. It would be three more days, on February the sixteenth when he would arrive. It was an easy delivery, seventeen hours of labor, but in a military hospital with only my girlfriend by my side, his Daddy off at war.

God was merciful and brought him home so the two could meet, I had done my job and delivered him and protected him and kept the home fires burning. Yet that was almost not enough. There was a period of transition that was not very peaceful at all; it was not exactly what I had anticipated. I put on my best jeans and dressed up, made a poster and brought our son waving his American flag and our new baby in the front pack to meet his Daddy. I was shaking like a leaf waiting for that plane to land. I couldn't wait for the two of them to meet, so I could be relieved of duty! I was proud to say, "Daddy, meet your son." And the tears flowed down for both of us.

But war can change a man. He was moody. He was in solitude. I was actively engaged in taking care of our toddler and our newborn – the one who had cried many nights when his Daddy was gone, and, the one who cried still, waiting for his Daddy to show up in his world. After three days of this awkwardness and disconnection, after three days of waiting for it to naturally transpire, for him to jump in and love on his son, I firmly said, "Enough. Here's your son, go figure it out." He started by giving him a bath and it was the beginning of their bond, but it took me saying, "Enough!"

It was a rocky re-entry and it was on again, off again like that for a time. We never really had time to settle in and adjust. Six months later, we would get the call that my Daddy had died unexpectedly in his sleep of a heart attack. I was my daddy's peanut, his shadow and my daddy's little girl. It was so hard; his mother – my grandmother, had just died in February. I couldn't possibly be losing my daddy. I was just 26. Girls need their Daddy. It had been about a month since I had spoken to him, which was very unusual, we usually spoke much more frequently. During our last call, he had me sing *Little Bunny Fu Fu*; he thought it was the cutest song and it entertained him. We laughed our heads off during that call; what a funny conversation. I didn't want him to be gone and I regretted it had been so long between calls.

We were just about to pull away from the house when we got the phone call that my daddy had died suddenly in his sleep. My husband always wanted to be a fixed wing pilot, even though he loved flying rotors as a helicopter pilot. We talked about it often; I kept encouraging him and finally decided we just had to make it a priority to make it happen. "You have to go," I just decided one day. His uncle was going to teach him if we could just get up to Ohio for the lessons, so we took a week of requested leave time, packed up the children and car fully loaded, we were about to pull away from the house. God was gracious to have us already packed and ready for a trip so in my grief I wouldn't have to attend to that.

The news was a shock and it was a very traumatic time for me.

We went immediately to the funeral instead of in the direction of the flying lessons scheduled in Ohio. I was still recovering from the funeral when about two weeks later my husband had to leave me for NRTC field training. That was a hard goodbye. I wasn't ready to be alone in my grief caring for a six month old and a two year old. They wanted their daddy and so did I – both their daddy and mine.

During NRTC, about two weeks in, my grandfather died. His wife – my grandmother- had just died in February and now him. A part of my family history was gone. No more connection to New York City and very few left to connect me to my daddy. I mourned deeply, but I just wasn't up for driving two young children without a husband to help, to New York City from Kentucky. I was sad about not being able to go to the funeral, but I just wasn't ready to mourn again; I was still grieving my Dad.

And for that matter, I was mourning the husband who wasn't home, yet again, after a nine month deployment to war. He was off on a three week training; it didn't make sense, I couldn't depend on him being home even during critical times like these. His transition from Desert Storm wasn't immediate and we were still grieving that separation as much as the reintegration. It was simply a very tumultuous year.

Six weeks later still my Uncle Tony in New York City died suddenly from a heart attack. I used to spend summers hanging out with his children, my cousins, at his house and getting to know him, often putting down a greasy New York pizza slice. I was recovering from a war that I didn't understand and my husband and I were struggling to stay bonded as a family with so many gaps in time and intimacy. It was life, it was the military, and it was our experience – a defining year.

We finished that year with new PCS orders, for a permanent change of duty station to Germany. As much as I was looking forward to the adventure, I hoped to have orders stateside where I could be close to my family to recover and as we were welcoming babies into our family.

Along with my hopes for the support of family, there too went my hopes of a career, yet again. In between the turmoil, I had tried to plug in as best I could as a Tupperware manager. Within six weeks I had twelve recruits. I went to weekly meetings and my unit was one of the highest performing units in our area. After four short months I had to say goodbye to my Tupperware unit so we could pack up our household goods and head to Germany to support the mission. This had just happened at our last duty station.

I had just finished training to become a certified image consultant for Color Me Beautiful a then popular cosmetic and color line. I was an independent sales consultant in Alabama when we were at Fort Rucker, the second half of flight school after we were just married following my stint as a newspaper reporter and my cookbook endeavor. I was regional sales manager for CMB servicing a chain of large department stores, then we got orders to Fort Campbell just after I closed three major locations in six weeks time. I attempted to continue independently offering color sessions to some of the officer's wives when we got to Fort Campbell, but it was too much of a challenge to pursue with no support on the home front when he was deployed and no nearby department stores . At Fort Rucker, after newspaper writing and before Color Me Beautiful training, I did quite a bit of substitute teaching which afforded me more flexibility around the Army's demand for my husband's time. It was later at Fort Campbell I found my way into a good position for the Public Affairs Office as a newspaper editor for the military community. I loved having that position as it was a quasi civilian position for a military community; it was an environment where I fit in and my skills had a purpose. Along the way there were career sacrifices supporting his aviation career, but there were benefits, too.

My favorite benefit was the travel involved–never for field training or deployments, of course, but it was available to us when he was taking transitional aviation courses or additional instruction, that the kids and I could go with him. Following our move from Fort Campbell to overseas, he had a six month school at Huachuca, Arizona. Since we have to clear the installation before heading to the next one, the children and I were packed and ready to go with him. We lived six weeks on Fort Huachuca and as he was busy in school, I fell in love with the state. My husband went to his class every morning from about eight thirty to three thirty and during that time I must have watched one hundred repetitions of The Jungle Book as my second son fell in love with Mowgli. My first son wanted to see 101 Dalmatians and I was seeing spots by the end of the day, stuck in a hotel room with two small, rambunctious boys, while their daddy was in class.

The moment he got home I would say, "We're getting in the car right now, we've got places to see and explore in Arizona." We visited Sedona, Tucson and even the Grand Canyon with the baby in the front pack and the oldest in the backpack. It was a great way to see so much of a new state we might not have otherwise gotten to.

Together we crossed the border and went to Nogales, New Mexico and collected some pottery and Mexican blankets which would become treasured mementos from our military travels. This was a benefit of being a military spouse. We got to take in new sights and collect beautiful souvenirs from different spots; mementos that our children would grow up taking to school year after year for show and tell. My travel book of memories was growing and I loved every moment of it.

But the frustration and anger was already taking seed and growing roots in my husband. It was the stress of having demands of a family and balancing the needs of the job. The boys and I were confined in a hotel and just anxious to break free when he got out of class. Learning a new aircraft was likely stressful and it caused him frustration trying to balance class and family and mission that trip. He didn't seem to know how to split his attention between studying for class and entertaining us and while he was agreeable to the daily side trips, I don't know if he was as eager to go some days as we were.

My children were little, but I was already thinking ahead to their future and I had received information on the Florida Pre-Paid college savings plan and determined that my children would go to college. I was already making a firm case as to why we were going to invest in this program.

As the first of seven children to go to college, I was fortunate to have a degree thanks to a college scholarship I earned through the America's Junior Miss program. I knew had it not been for that scholarship, I might not have had the opportunity. There was no money put aside for my education, with seven kids there were many other demands. It was a grace from God that I earned that scholarship. I wanted my children to have college as part of their future and scholarships notwithstanding, I knew we'd have to provide it with careful planning. I pitched it to my husband, but all he could see was a military paycheck that could not support this goal that was so far off in the future.

It was a big argument for a little hotel. In the end, I won the argument and we started the prepaid program in the two boys' names, but I was beginning to lose the battle because the tension was increasing between us as we travelled that day. It was especially evident as we traveled through Tombstone walking about the old town and encountering Doc Holliday's tombstone was like walking around waiting for a gunfight.

As I tried to take in the sights, there was really chaos that day. My husband was showing a face I had never seen before. It was a new mix of tension–residue of war and probably anticipation of what lie ahead, traveling overseas with his family, planning for their future, not sure of how to even attend to their needs today. How would he manage it, the stress and the unanswered questions, I'm not sure what his struggles were, but it was evident during this trip.

For me, moving overseas was going to be an adventure. I was only stressed about leaving my family at a time when I had small babies; I wanted each to know the relationships of extended families, grandmas and cousins alike. I was excited about going overseas.

We did enjoy a great family vacation, all four of us tucked into a one bedroom efficiency, in the beautiful state of Arizona while my husband managed to complete his military schooling, but it was very stressful and at great emotional cost. We had no control, no choice to go or decline the course or the separation that not going would have brought or the closing of our former quarters. We couldn't just pack up our bags and leave him to finish the course – we were a very long way from any family, so when the anger bubbled up and the kids got zoo-ey, we couldn't just pack up and leave him to finish school, we were in it together. The military told us we had to be there and there we were. We had to make our way around it. That's how it would be at every one of our duty stations and nearly every time we traveled with him for training.

It was a lot to keep up with packing, moving; packing, travelling; packing, unpacking – there was a lot of baggage with kids, a wife and a soldier. Plus the children wanted to be in constant motion and we had to be in confined quarters, making it additionally stressful.

At the EH-60 transition training course at Fort Huachuca, Arizona, it just made sense to go by car so we could pack the kids in and have a way around for sightseeing. The problem is we took my husband's original Oldsmobile Cutlass Supreme with over 165,000 miles on the engine. He loved that car. He didn't want to part with it for anything, much to my chagrin. And then the inevitable happened, we were headed south to Florida at the end of a training day, dusk was setting in, light rain began to fall and BAM! The engine dropped, right there on the side of the road with our most precious cargo – two babies in their car seats and no relief in sight. It poured down pressure and stress and responsibility into my husband's bucket, already over flowing from the burdens of a family in his military world.

Again, we were under God's covering because as the story would go, the engine dropped while we were driving on a desolate part of the interstate not half a mile from a Department of Transportation sign that warned motorists to not pick up hitch hikers because we were in a state penitentiary zone. The driver said he only stopped because of the military uniform. He took us to the nearest exit about 30 miles down the road where we would find very questionable lodging and negotiate ourselves into a new (used) vehicle to finish our trip. Another financial burden added to the list. But a family needs a car and it was the cheapest mode of transportation back to Florida.

All the way, hundreds and hundreds of miles and hours and hours of driving we drove to South Florida where my husband would leave me and our two sons to go overseas to our next duty post. They call it 'going ahead'.

We had our hold baggage with us – two suitcases a piece to last us in the transition of the move until the remaining household goods arrived, about three months later. Eventually, I had to bring our car to port early, too. It would be another six weeks after we arrived in Germany that our new car would arrive, as well. We were at the mercy of my mother and my family in the gap time. The two kids and I went to stay with her in her one bedroom apartment. My mom and I quietly celebrated Korey's first birthday with a cake.

My husband went overseas ahead of us to live in housing units for military soldiers who were married but not yet accompanied. He also went ahead to accept housing quarters for us.

During that period of waiting time until we would join him, I had such challenges managing those two little active boys of our. For example, my strong-willed eighteen month old was now coming up on his second birthday. One day he was behind the wheel of the car in the driver's seat while I waited for my mother to come out of her apartment and join us in the car. My pregnant belly was starting to protrude and there was barely room for him to squeeze in front of me while we waited. It was time for me to put him in his car seat and I tried to release the grip he had on the steering wheel but I could not manage to get him loose. I slid out of the car and tried to get a better approach, but try as I might, I could not pull the grip of his hands off the steering wheel.

I struggled fiercely, my mother slid into the car with us on the passenger's side, the two adults could not get this nearly two year old off the steering wheel; he was determined to drive the car. He said he wanted to drive the car to go see his daddy. It was not so adorable as we were dripping in the hot Florida sun and were helpless to overcome this little squirt. Fortunately, I saw a police officer patrolling the parking lot and asked for his assistance. It took the three adults to get his hands off the steering wheel. It was moments like that that I really wished there had been a daddy around.

Then there was a night when I woke up in the middle of the night to my second child wheezing. The pre-term labor had taken its toll, his lungs were well-developed but they rarely got full oxygenation. He was probably in the low ninety percent range and so sometimes he struggled with full breathing.

This particular night he woke up and his lungs rattled, and I didn't understand what it was. Was it asthma? It was certainly wheezing and there was a rattling. I probably should have gone to the emergency room, but I didn't know where to go. I was at my mother's home and I didn't really know the area. That was a common plight of constant travelling and moving, always asking where the emergency room was located; I promise it would come up in an emergency every time we didn't ask.

I just remember holding him from three o'clock in the morning through the dark of the night, until the sun would rise the next morning. I prayed over him, I held him and I cried with him. I prayed for his struggle and I wished that his daddy had been there to help me through that scary night. Gratefully, his wheezing subsided by sunrise and the prescription cough medicine that I had given him eventually helped give him relief.

There were many moments like this as a mother, trying to raise children, that I would really dread the job and the moves and the demands; these were the times, I just wanted support, someone else to cry with me and help with the rocking and tell me things were going to be okay.

There would be a lot of parenting challenges as I was a military spouse, many of them involving doctors and medical issues I had to face alone. When I arrived in Germany, in fact, we would find ourselves in the emergency room on more than one occasion.

When he left for Germany, I was still wearing my fitting blue jeans and when I arrived overseas, I would be close to wearing maternity clothes. Shortly after he left, I learned I was pregnant, but kept it a secret until my arrival overseas. We would be welcoming our third child as began anew in Germany.

The plane ride alone with two toddlers overseas was challenging in itself. I had to have a diaper bag for each of the children so I could have a supply of things to entertain them. Forget that it would be a long flight for me due to my early pregnancy. I didn't know what to expect for quarters, but everything seemed to be a shock at first. When I arrived, I didn't expect to see the quarters so stark. It was like living in a sterile clinic. Everything was white, everything had a clean space, but everything was sterile and tile and white.

The floors were cold. The two flights of stairs were open stairs and I thought of the safety hazard for my two toddlers. It was a beautiful two story home with a basement, even though the basement was cold and unfinished, it would become a play space for my children. I would adjust to the sterile quarters, grateful for the spaciousness and the cul de sac location it offered.

I was fighting the urge to return to the United States, but I knew I would soon acclimate to being so far away in the world and to our new home. In those first few days we would sit on the cul-de-sac out in front of the home on a bench, where all the wives would gather while my husband was at work. I was in this new place and still trying to get over my jet lag; I had to entertain the two children and ignore the nausea my pregnancy was causing.

Sitting on the bench this early afternoon, one of the children's bicycle collided right into my toddler on a neighbor's tricycle, amongst all the other children at play. Sure enough, Korey was quickly crying and it was evident he was going to need stitches. I ran to him and I knew instantly we had to find our way to an emergency room – Murphy's Law, I think. But I had just arrived in Germany. I was still jet- lagged, I didn't even know where I was! I didn't yet know my house number. I didn't know my phone number. Everything took an international code, making it even more difficult to remember. I didn't even know who to call. I didn't even know my husband's unit. We hadn't been in-country long enough to rehearse any of these details.

I didn't know how to reach my husband yet because he had said he would call *me* on his lunch hour. Where would I go? I didn't speak the language. All these questions flew threw my head as I was grasping at ways to gain control of the situation. Where was the closest hospital? Thankfully, within minutes the wife next to me had come to my rescue. She had been in the country for more than six months and she knew where to take me and the answers to all those other important questions. We arrived for stitches with both children in tow, not speaking the language, but thankfully, we didn't need a language, my son's bleeding knee and forehead did the talking for us.

The doctors were very generous and offered very good service and kind smiles. They tried to calm me, they could see my fears, and somehow, eventually, we were able to reach my husband's unit and give him information that we were at the hospital.

It wouldn't be the first time Korey would have stitches; he would run into walls that didn't move, he would run into bleachers and need stitches, he would roll down the hill and end up in the bottom of a 15 foot ditch and need retrieving. One time he needed staples in his head when he ran into the wall of a hotel room. He was just that kind of kid: playful, boisterous, physical, jumping, moving, not knowing that everything didn't yield to his contact. He was just all 'boy'. I was thankful for that military wife who came to my aid that day. I would have to lean on the wives often while we were overseas because my husband was often duty committed.

In spite of two toddlers and a growing belly, I was going to need something more. I was going to need a job. How would I engage? I didn't speak the language and had no idea how I'd get around, but I figured I would worry about those details later. I was going find a job one way or another. Thankfully, within weeks, I heard of a position in the military community where my experiences as a newspaper reporter would come in handy.

I was so happy to be there, but it sure did take some persistence to get to work. Neither our car or our household goods had yet arrived. Even in May and into June in Germany you need coats, gloves, scarves and boots, and it would be a harsh Winter until Summer finally arrived in July. We were not prepared for this weather and would depend on family to expedite a box of warm gear for us.

I was going to need it as I would walk several blocks to the first bus stop down the street our neighborhood. I would take the bus to a depot that was a holding terminal and I would walk from there to the Kaserne or the military community, that was still another twelve blocks away.

Once there, it was a climb of three flights of stairs of old billets that would become my office. I was happy to do it. I was healthy, this was a joyful pregnancy and Germany was a beautiful place to walk about, the transit was all easy enough to access. But one certainly had to be dedicated and committed and bundled up to make it happen. It helped that I found a great job in media relations serving the Army community.

CHAPTER FIVE

DREAMS REALLY DO COME TRUE–A LIFE OF BENEFITS

There are so many benefits being in the military like travel, travel, travel; even when you have to travel in jump seats. I remember a time when we wanted to go back to the United States to visit our families for Thanksgiving. We had to do it in a C130.

No problem, because we only paid a boarding fee of about eighteen dollars per person and it was even less for the children so the entire family flew for about $100. So what if we had to do cross the ocean in jump-seats to make it stateside again. The seats were made of cording or netting woven together. So, it wasn't so much like first class seats on Delta. And, no, we didn't get any peanuts on this flight.

But that was okay. I was thrilled to be traveling home to see my family. We had to wait for an undetermined time, sometimes a full day, in the terminal of the Mac flights and wait to see if we made the flight because there was a system to the wait, based on seniority and when you signed up and what your priority was.

One time we were on a MAC flight (Military Air Command), travelling to the states and there was a loss of cabin pressure. It was a little unnerving as the masks actually came down in the cabins and we had to put them over our faces. Everything turned out fine, it was a minor technicality that was quickly resolved and we made it to our destination with our eighteen dollar tickets and some in-air entertainment to talk about.

We didn't even have to travel anywhere, living in Germany you can see so many beautiful and unique things. Markets are always interesting and lively. Markets on Wednesdays, markets on Saturdays; you can have fresh fruit any season from the market. My first experience was buying fresh cherries. The gentlemen put the plump cherries into an ice cream, paper cone. There were two handfuls of cherries and it cost eight Deutsche Marks, that was a little over $6, which I thought was quite expensive, but they were worth every moment of the experience.

How exciting to walk through a market popping plump cherries in my mouth. There would also be the little carts of fruits and veggies that would go through the communities. The peddlers would ring their bells, much like an ice cream truck vendor in the states. You would run out and they would lift the sides of their vending trucks much like garage doors and there would be a surprising array of fresh fruits.

Inside there would be baskets and baskets of fresh fruits and vegetables. And fresh candies, too. There were always a variety of candies to entertain the children while you would pick out which pieces of fruit you wanted to take home.

Beyond fruits and vegetables you could find local treasure during 'junking days.' If you were really ready for some interesting finds, you could rummage through the treasures during spermuhle. Once a month you would go around the community and people would put all of the things they didn't want on the street side. It would be like a yard sale, only nothing was for sale, but rather free for the taking. You would just go through other people's junk, so to speak, quickly making them your own treasures.

There would be purses, dressers and even wardrobes and larger pieces of furniture. There would be things they didn't want to keep in their home as I understood it, because it was tax season and a wardrobe was a large wooden closet and you were taxed for how many closets you had in your home.

Free was good; we collected some treasures on these days. Plus, I loved that you would walk around and get to know your German friends and neighbors. It was a fun ritual. The locals were happy for us to take their things, but they mostly thought it was strange that Americans considered these disposed items as treasures. After spermuhle then, there would be antiquing on the weekends.

There would be these fabulous flea markets the size of fairgrounds. They would be roasting up succulent mushrooms which were battered and deep fried and there would be a lovely sauce you put on the side of a paper boat. For about eight marks, you could have a delicious snack as you walked around antique shopping.

My favorite treasure still is an old, beautiful, porcelain soup tureen that I have spent many holidays making soup for and we have presented it on our family table for many events. I have treasured this soup tureen that I had found at one of the beautiful antique markets in Germany. Another favorite treasure was a large ornamental crucifix : a wooden cross, hand crafted, with stories to tell, but stories I will never know.

It must have come out of a war-torn church some-where that had been bombed, I can only imagine. Surely, it had come out of a church where it sat in a prominent space so beautiful, but now I hang it in every foyer of every house I move to. This cross is a beautiful reminder of my time in Germany, a beautiful reminder of my Christ on the cross and of my faith. I have stood before, knelt before and prayed before this cross on many occasions.

With tears streaming down my face I have prayed for my soldier's return, prayed for my family's needs, for their souls, their salvation, their future and their future spouses and thought and reflected on my hopes and my dreams, my losses and my triumphs and many times my marriage. This cross is very meaningful to me and one of the treasures that I collected overseas.

My time overseas was very special and chock full of memories. I enjoyed so many fun experiences in Germany and all of these activities lead to treasures and travel memories which I hold dear. One of the benefits of traveling is that family members can come visit and are further encouraged by the opportunity for travel.

My cousin Liz who was in education and had the summer off came to see me. I was happy to take her around Germany, it was an excuse for me to get out and experience more of little towns like Rothenberg, more lunches, spermuhling and introducing her to a culture and a nature that I was new to her.

Another time, my sister came over with her new husband and honeymooned in Italy and Germany. I helped her plan a great trip because I had already had the benefit of visiting Italy and could recommend places in Germany, as well. My brother came with his wife and was able to pick out a grandfather clock from the Black Forest that he treasures still today. And my mother has said her fondest memories are the times she came to Germany and we travelled together. These are the benefits of the Army that are priceless.

The greatest benefit was the travel I got to experience. In spite of not having a treasure trove of travel funds, I was able to fully take advantage of every opportunity to travel. Having been to more than thirty countries before we finally said, "Auf wiedersehen" to the country that had opened up its home to my children and my family, I had a pretty full passport as an added bonus of our overseas duty post. Travel, travel and more travel was the best benefit of military life overseas. My single mother was able to come over on many occasions for three months, six months and up to nine months at a time; there was no restriction from the Army and it was very helpful for us.

My husband wanted to make her a dependent so she could stay permanently and while she came to stay on several occasions, we never pursued the dependent status. While she was there, my mother would watch the children while I worked, Monday through Friday. Then on the weekends my husband would watch the children while she and I would travel to many different countries. She would learn to speak some of the language, like when she went to order *coffee, brotchen and bratwurst mit senf.*

She would love the nature of the German folks and talk infectiously about her experiences often. She would love all of the experience she had, a gift she could never experience as a single mother or as a waitress on a waitress salary, but as a benefit of the military life we supported. It was a gift that we could share with her. We enjoyed many travel experiences and became very close as mother and daughter, making up for some of the lost time when I was little and she was working to support me and not able to spend much time with me.

There were many times when my husband and children traveled with us and we went as a family. We had many great experiences on the Mediterranean. We got to travel to Italy – a lifelong dream for all of us due to our Italian family heritage. I kissed the ground when we arrived.

I was grateful that my mother could be there to experience these amazing travel journeys and life with my children in tow. That was important to our family. We called her Noni, an Italian version of grandmother–Nonna, Noni. Everyone from family to friends of family called her Noni. It was an Italian tradition.

My children grew very close to her and I was grateful for the home that the military allowed us to make for her as our guest. We experienced so many milestones in the military: my son's birthday, my daughter's first birthday; my mother was there to help create a beautiful first birthday. A first birthday tea, where all of the mothers on the block brought their highchairs of their daughters, of their children, and we had a mother daughter tea. All of these memories and life moments were exactly what I wanted for my children and my mother. Even though we were far from home due to his military career, some of the loss was redeemed when we were able to have her in our home for longs periods of time and opportunities to travel.

Noni was there to help with Kaitlin's first birthday party where we served petit fours, caviar toast and hot tea. Instead of silver service, there were baby bottles and baby food and all of the perfect appointments that celebrated Kaitlin's birthday as a princess in the land of princesses and princes. We announced our children's births with, "Hear ye, hear ye! All ye of the land!" And we called ourselves King and Queen and our children Princess and Prince. We announced that in play, not because we were royalty, but because we live in the land of castles and there was a certain royal air about that as we heralded the births of each of our children. Definitely a fun thing to balance out all the inconvenience to come from change of duty stations.

Another benefit was the welcoming environment at work. Everyone understood the hardships involved in overseas duty including limited access to grandma and babysitters. For this reason, I was able to bring Kaitlin to work with me in her car seat when she was only three days old. It was fun carrying her into the board room where I was the director of marketing and had a board meeting, showing her off and thinking of how this might impact her future. I knew she would go on to do great things, if her first outing was at a conference meeting.

There were perks to being overseas, but, then again, there were some inconveniences, little ones like dealing with no television, no television stations and no cartoons to entertain the kids; not that that is a great loss, I don't really prefer TV, but for children they can sometimes be entertained by it.

But that's okay, we watched Disney video after Disney video and Barney, Captain Kangaroo, Dora and all of the Disney videos became my children's friends and my children's teachers.

Who needed a breakfast of non-stop American cartoons, anyway. We had more unique ways to enjoy breakfasts. My husband couldn't wait to greet me that first day off of the airplane with German brotchen, butterkase cheese, fresh-cut salamis and pear juice out of a glass decanter.

He had gone to the German butchery and had hand selected things for me that were very representative of our local area and he set the table and there we had our first taste of Germany. We would have many of these while in our little community or on the road on our travels. The most common breakfast would be a brotchen, or a hard roll, with butter and sometimes with cheese, butterkase being our favorite.

We would have a boiled egg or a soft poached egg, and sometimes berries, like himbeer (raspberries), and jam on our rolls. There were interesting things and treats to taste, and we were being introduced to it all. Often times we would take an exit on the Autobahn, the interstate in Germany, and we would stop and see what was in the nearest market. For breakfast we would find something along the way and there would always be peppermint tea, chamomile tea, hard rolls, cheese and meats. Traveling was definitely the greatest benefit of military service.

We had lots of unique experiences during our travels. One time my mother and I were on the Autobahn in our fuel injected car and were close to being out of gas. Now, we had to buy gas in rations; the military was given books and you could only have so much gas per month.

I had my ration book with me, but there was no gas station in sight. We were in Holland, having a fantastic time having just seen windmills on a dyke, having just driven up the coast on our way back from the Rotterdam; we were having an amazing experience. Then all of a sudden, so it seemed, we found ourselves in the middle of nowhere in a non-populated area.

We were two women in the middle of nowhere with no gas and I was in charge. We were driving along and in slow motion realized we were not in a safe place anymore. It wasn't like I could pick up the phone and call anyone. First of all, I had no cell phone then. Second of all, my husband was in another country. I was in Holland and he was in Germany. We didn't know how to speak this Dutch language. There were plenty of English speaking folks, but none were around as this was happening, in fact, there was no one around to ask for help at all.

We were absolutely in a deserted, desolate area. I started to panic, I started to lose control. I was definitely overwhelmed and nearly hyperventilating. My mother was very nervous, trying to calm me down. "Jacqueline, it will be ok! Jacqueline, we will find a gas station!" But what would happen when my fuel injected car ran out of gas? My husband had always told me this was a big deal. Who would come and rescue us? There was no AAA, there were no helicopters in sight – as if my husband would just fly over and come to the rescue–no, we would be on our own.

Shortly after all of this was transpiring and I was still able to make forward movement on this road, in spite of running on fumes, miracles of all miracles, there was a gas station that came in sight. I truly believe I rolled into the gas station as the buzzer went off that the gas was completely out of my car. We were so grateful to be there and had barely escaped that peril.

We had so many unique experiences in our travels, not many as stressful as that one. Often times when my mother and I are sitting around the family table we will bring them up and relive them. It is so much fun to think that our passports have stamps from Italy, to Poland, to Holland, to Germany.

It's amazing to think that from our modest home in South Florida, we have experienced all of this wonderful travel, all because of the military. One time we were in Aviano, Italy, planning to sleep on the military posts where the quarters were much, much cheaper and affordable than a local pension.

When we arrived it was a hot, sticky night, we had three children with us, my husband and my mother, and there were no sleeping quarters available. They did offer a barracks divided between men and women where one of us could sleep. So my husband went with the boy babies to sleep in one bed and my mother and I went into the other.

There was a woman snoring so loudly, we decided to take refuge in our car. We ended up sleeping in the car with the windows cracked all night on this hot, sticky night.

In the morning my husband went to take the babies to the bathroom to freshen up and I was in the car with my mother. I am very modest and I had to change clothes after that sticky night in the car, but we didn't know where the women's room was. My mother encouraged me to just change my shirt in the car.

After much cajoling I decided I could possibly do it if I was very, very quick. I took off my shirt, quickly attempted to put on my other one. I couldn't quite get it over my head and in the process I was appalled to see paratroopers floating through the sky just above the car.

Now, only on a military base would you find this. I was aghast and quickly put on my shirt. I am sure nothing was revealed, but it was a silly little experience–who would have expected–and a memory that we talk about often.

We had so many good memories in Germany between travelling and working. I was on top of the world and it was definitely a highlight of my life. My career was going great. I had progressed from a media coordinator, to a marketing director, to the chief of marketing in short order due both to hard work and other people moving on with change of duty stations.

I was now managing women and a staff of other satellite offices and was part of an organization bigger than me. I was known as the "go to gal" for customer service, service excellence and for customer service standards. I was loving that part of my life; collaborating with all of the top leaders of the community. I had financial flow with a regular paycheck and my husband was doing fine in his career.

I had a great job in the military community, but there were hardships. As a working mom I still had all of the same challenges of all working moms. I had to find daycare for my children when my mother was not there visiting. I preferred the in home daycare experience over the post daycare experience. I didn't want my child in a preschool picking up germs in a facility while I was at work.

I often relied on neighbors or home daycare settings. Penny was a dear friend who took care of five children; my heart went out to her. Every day that I left my Kyle, he would beat on the door as soon as I closed it. He would cry and the temper tantrum would start; he didn't want me to go.

He had huge separation anxiety and I would cry and be sad but we would close that glass door as a barrier between us and she would reassure me, "He will be fine! He always stops after you get off to work."

It tore at my heart, but I wanted to go to work and I needed to go to work. A military paycheck is not very big and we had a growing family with lots of dreams and goals and demands. My son would have to learn to stay home and thankfully, he was loved by a caring military spouse.

My babies were growing and I was a mother with three children, at that point, and a career. I was enjoying the power and freedom that came from that. This was during the first part of our Germany tour. We had been enjoying all the benefits of travel, a position in the military community and even a few accolades.

My marketing position put me in a position of leadership where I would welcome VIP visitors and promote the community facilities. I was responsible for a large-scale military community marathon where we welcomed both German and American runners. I was meeting many people in the community. As a result, I was called to be a representative of my community when it was time for the community to draw down, or close, due to funding and mission changes.

In the States we have Mardi Gras, and in Germany we have similar festivities called Fasching.

I was asked to be the Fasching Princezzen to represent the community. As such, my military husband would become the Fasching Prince. I would be the princess and he would be the prince. This was so fitting and we were honored to be asked.

For six weeks we went around to other military communities and the German communities and represented the American Kaserne. We had a travelling group which consisted of a dance team, a colonel, the post theatre director and other top officials and this formed our American team.

The Germans thought we were celebrities as we travelled around saying "Auf Wiedersehen" on behalf of our military kaserne which was soon to close. The German communities also had representatives from their various small towns. They wore the same tuxedos and the same ball gown to every event. The military folks wore their uniforms and the dance team their dance uniforms. I had quite the wardrobe of 'After Five' evening gowns and short cocktail dresses from my pageant days and was able to wear something new at every event. They took this to mean I was a celebrity and I seemed to receive extra attention as a result.

They often commented that my husband and I were smashing on stage and they often encouraged him to linger and hold the mic and sing. One night I found myself in the parking lot wondering what was taking him so long to join me as we were departing and heading to our waiting van. He had been detained and was still inside singing *Country Roads, Take Me Home*, which he was encouraged to sing and for which he received a standing ovation from the German crowd.

We received many medals from each community in attendance and often times, heartfelt gifts of tremendous ten pound logs of salami that were homemade. These revelers were farmer s in their community or business people welcoming us and showing us honor as we represented as ambassadors of the American military community. They were big-hearted folks and rolled out the red carpet of hospitality for us. It was a privilege to act as ambassadors for our American community and to be hosted in such a way. We probably attended 30 events in six weeks time. It was an amazing experience.

It was also during this time I was able to bring my theatre career back to life and I auditioned for the role of Shelby, in Steel Magnolias. It was a full length theatre production put on for the military families. We had a wonderful theatre director who put his heart and energy into a great production and filling the house every night. There was such an active theatre community throughout the military posts in Europe that they hosted an awards program that imitated the likes of the Emmys, the Grammys, the Tony Awards – it was a festive gathering to honor those involved in military theatre in the European community.

They honored actors in several categories such as best actress, best leading lady, best supporting actresses and so forth. It was much to my surprise that I was honored as the best leading actress for my role as Shelby, in Steel Magnolias. It was like living my dream. It had slightly redeemed the fact that I had never made it to the American Academy of Dramatic Arts in New York City, although I had auditioned and been accepted, but turned down pursuing it to marry my military man and follow his career.

It somewhat made up for the lost dream and, I thought it ironic, that Julia Roberts had played the role of Steel Magnolias in the film version, and I had won this award in the theatre version overseas in the European market. Julia Roberts always being an actress I looked up to and a graduate of a theatre school in New York, too, I believe. I always teased she got all my roles – the ones I was never able to audition for.

After all of this joy, now having three children, many travel memories and just enjoying the benefits of an overseas tour, my husband also was enjoying his career as a helicopter pilot, a new mood set in.

One fall as we were laying in bed, my husband shocked me and simply announced, "I'm not happy."

I thought, *how could that be? I am the happiest I have ever been–I have been Cinderella to the ball, I have worn gowns and been given medals, we were celebrities! How could you not be happy? You are in your chosen career, we are in the land of castles, we have three beautiful children, we are all thriving, and you're not happy?*

It was completely out of left field to me and I was confused. All I knew was to respond. I set out to make him happy. I kept a calendar of all of the great things we did. I tried to please him in every way I knew. But nothing would seem to work. I didn't correlate it at the time, but other things were going on in the bigger picture. There was a lot of unrest in our community. Soon the community would close down and that announcement had had a jarring affect on everyone. The Fulda gap where we were stationed had been a favored and meaningful post for both Germans and Americans alike.

I reflected on where we were at that time. There was a particular defining moment beyond that moment where he told me he was not happy. It occurred right about that time on a trip to Spain. My mother was in-country and watched the children while we were to go away. He and I went to Spain to enjoy some time by ourselves for a week, and during the trip, we seemed to be having a fine time but there was some tension about holding each other's hands.

Whose hand should be on top, whose hand should be on the bottom, should fingers be interlocked or not? I didn't understand it. He seemed to be grumbling a lot. We were more combative than we were enjoying our time but we were taking in the wonders of the city and still having a grand time, making the most of our gift of time away.

And then a moment that could not be undone occurred. We were out on the veranda enjoying Sangria in the early hours of the evening. Dusk was setting in and we were sitting at a white plastic bistro table and we were situated outside on the cobblestone. We were chatting about our trip but we were getting inwardly somber and it was starting to permeate the air. I brought up the fact that he had said he was not happy and was asking what could I do.

"I'm just not happy," he said. "You have added no value to my life and I don't know what we are going to do about it." I literally fell off my chair. I don't know how it happened, the plastic leg must have gotten twisted in the cobblestone, but I literally fell to the ground. I was in such shock.

I had given him three beautiful children, then four, two and one years of age. I was a productive, working woman and had cash coming in the house. I cooked home-made meals from scratch: biscuits and gravy, even the egg rolls and fried rice! I was a good mother, I was a good wife; I was happy when he came home at night, we spent lots of our time traveling. How could he not be happy?

Little did I know that the seed of happiness was deep in him and I would never be able to satisfy it. It probably was bubbling up from many deployments, from having spent many Thanksgivings alone in the military, from having already been deployed time after time, from seeing me travel with my mother and him not being able to be a part of that because he was busy with his military commitments or staying behind to care for the children.

Maybe he was even impacted still from the loss of not having been there during our second child's birth;

maybe from carrying the weight of all of the stress of the military commitment and life around. Probably from not being the husband that he wanted to be, or the parent that he wanted to be because he was limited by his commitment to the military. I can't answer where this seed of sadness came from.

Maybe it was from the anxiety of the tour ahead and the sadness of closing the post. Maybe it was the sadness of goodbyes of all of the frivolity as Fasching princess and prince. Or, in the sadness of his heart, he didn't want to say goodbye to what he already knew at this duty station.

Maybe it was the uncertainty of wondering why he had brought his wife and these beautiful children, this family he loved, into an environment of chaos and uncertainty. Or maybe that was me making excuses and truly, maybe he was just not happy. Truly, just maybe I wasn't bringing value to his life or his idea of family. Only he can answer these questions to solve the puzzle of our lives.

There were other things that came on the tail of this; duty station and a community under pressure. There would be three significant events in the Aviation community. One was a situation of infidelity and a murder-suicide, another involved a decapitation of a soldier with grisly details. It rocked the community and left a darkness that hung as we were left with the responsibility of closing the community. He as an aviator and me as a marketing community leader, we were left to attend to the community and to prepare the facilities for closure. The third event was the abuse of a child which resulted in her eventual death. He was the soldier on duty to manage the details of that horrific and sad case that night.

My questions of his unhappiness would come before the community incidents. I had lingering questions that would stir deeply and loudly from his announcement that night and from our trip to Spain – questions that would linger and remain unanswered as we progressed to our next duty station.

It was a question that would take root and we would feed with our anger, our bitterness, our frustration and our unknowing. It was a question that life in the military would not support to finding a brilliant answer to, but would only add chaos as we continued to struggle, survive and thrive as we experienced life within its borders. Another duty station was not welcome news. After all the unrest, three years of German winters and isolation from family and our America, I was very ready to return stateside. Instead, the Army opted to move us to a new duty post a few hours south. We said goodbye to a post we loved, but with heavy hearts for what lie ahead.

CHAPTER SIX

A LIFE OF BENEFITS,
BUT AT WHAT COST?
BOTH LIFE AND CHAOS

As military life would have it, there was a lot of stress and constant pressure. The soldiers were constantly under stress working without the equipment they needed, especially during drawdown, working under budget restraints, working under uncertainty; would they deploy or not deploy?

They were always working under pressure, trying to perform better, maintain their physical training standards, whatever was needed so they would be prepared for their next review, their next rank promotion and

124

ultimately, the next dollar increase in their salary. There was always an uphill climb and always stress.

At home there was a degree of stress as well, mostly in the little things. For example, I might not be satisfied not finding the items I needed at the grocery to meet the needs of my meal planning or I'd complain that there wasn't an opportunity to make more money because finding a position after the transfer was quite challenging or express my frustrations that we couldn't be near our families. These frustrations were typical for other wives, too and other soldiers and families often complained about the very same things. Looking from the outside, it might sound whiny or spoiled, but military posts overseas were limited sometimes with supplies. For example, it's summer and you want to take your kids on a picnic and you want to bring a watermelon, either they are not available or they cost $8 or $12 and that's not in the budget, so you choose something else and after one or two times, you start longing for the fresh produce from your favorite Southern grocer or from the farmer's stand. And then you can't find your favorite this or that and your cosmetic line is discontinued and you have to wait until you drive an hour to the next post that still carries it and this affects nearly every item you consume or use on a regular basis. There is stress and consistent pressure from of all of the sacrifices that are required of the soldier and their family when they are deployed. The pressure mounts especially when everyone is waiting on orders for a new Permanent Change of Station (PCS). The entire family is on pins and needles as the military has their entire lives in balance and so many questions are waiting to be answered because they inevitable affect a laundry list of decisions to be made – should we invest in a new comforter for the bed that we just put up because the baby outgrew the crib, do we buy the new bike for her birthday or do we wait, what if we go back to the states instead of stay in-country and the list goes on.

And when we first arrived in country, there was stress as we learned to manage without our household goods and we waited for them to arrive on the slowest boat from China, or the U.S. We were always unsure of when they would arrive and how to react or plan for the in-between time. It's cold, do we go buy new coats for the entire family? When will the shipment arrive–maybe this week, maybe two more? The stress mounted with every event and every waiting order and compounded with every change and transition and people's emotions got all knotted up with the details of all the moves – not just us, military families experiencing military life just as we did. We were, after all, human beings responding to all of this stress and all we wanted was simple information on what our lives would look like on the other side of the orders. On the outside everyone was smiling, happy to know one another, always planning the next ball or the next dining-in or military function, looking forward to new duty stations and new adventures. That was the fun side, the benefit side of military life–always looking for ways to get together and celebrate, applaud one another's promotions, applaud one another's births, their growing family size, so long as the dress we packed arrived in time.

We were rocked by the horrible deaths I already mentioned. Sometimes, though, the pressures grew and spiraled and weren't manageable; it was a level of frustration from the constant pressures and inconveniences and unknowns that could no longer be swept under the welcome mat. This happened for us toward the end of our duty assignment in Fulda, we were a community under pressure and not just a family assigned to duty, but also leaders responsible for the morale, welfare and recreation of others assigned there and for representing the community when local nationals visited. There was a lot expected during this assignment and with the connection of community dwindling and drawing down, the stress was mounting and taking its toll.

The announcement had come one spring: Budget cuts and the post would close. Fulda was heralded as an important, strategic place on the border; a place where people remembered the days when the wall was up in Germany. The wall had long since crumbled, but there was crumbling on the military installation of another kind and chaos mounted from the community downsizing; the support that once existed was now gone.

In our own units we were rocked. A soldier had committed murder. Then there was a second incident: A soldier had been decapitated. We didn't understand this gruesome, horrible incident. In the units, the stress was paramount. Yes, there were counselors and still some family support teams, but often we didn't have access to the care and counseling or it wasn't enough. The soldiers and family members who were even more removed, were left in their confusion to continue as if life were normal; to make sure their units functioned at full capacity, as if there was no change, no shortage of staff or supplies. The military family was left also to learn to manage, but the only shopping opportunities we had were closing and slowly so were the outreach facilities. Groceries were being limited, things were inconsistent and unreliable. It caused a lot of stress in the home and it rippled through the community.

Just prior to this, my mother one day said, "Jackie, in spite of these three children and their constant activity, their constant mess in the house, you never raise your voice, you're not normal. You never get excited, you never get stressed. You just say *now children, let's not do that. Now, it's okay, tomorrow will be better.*"

That's how I truly was, nothing ruffled me. Then the stress of the military started seeping in and the stress from the unit came home. I'm sure each of these events played their own roles in wreaking havoc on us. Within months of her very words, there would no longer be peace in our home and the soldier would no longer be able to maintain his cool and there would be emotional explosions in the home with full force which would upset the serenity of our once peaceful home. Soon the norm would be a loss of patience, irrational behaviors and imposed discipline with the children and when there was not a noise, there would be a silence that said it all.

As we were preparing to move to our new duty station we had to clear our quarters and scrub and clean until it was spit shine polished. A soldier was expected to leave his quarters the way he learned to clean his barracks in boot camp. It was a great policy. We both believe in leaving things better than we found them, but this was a big house, a big move and we had little children.

I was in the car with the two little children asleep in their car seats and nursing the third, the moon was glowing in the sky and the night was dark, [It makes the verse to our wedding song *Stand By Me* run through my head. *When the Night is Dark and the moonlight is the only light you'll see. Darlin', Darlin' won't you Stand By Me.*]

I was standing by outside in the dark of the night taking care of the children, nursing a baby with two asleep in their car seats, while the soldier was on his hands and knees scrubbing the kitchen floor so that there would be a spit shine remaining and we could pass the inspection to clear quarters and make way to depart for our new duty station in Ansbach, Germany.

There were many moment like this when it was time to change duty stations. There was always lots of physical labor involved and the children still had to be cared for and time was always running out as we both had to cram in duties of the day and the job. And when it was time for inspection, it was simply time. All the tasks had to be done.

With less than a year left in our original orders, we fully expected and hoped to return stateside. The military almost always sends you back stateside that close out. But for whatever reason, the post in Ansbach was in greater need and we had no choice; our orders would be for a new assignment to continue on in Germany. There would be more opportunity for snow, scraping the ice off of our car windows to get to work, more time with our kids stuck in the confined quarters in the winter month after month. There would be more time away from our families–holiday after holiday, where we would not be around the table with them.

We would have no choice. The base was closing and we would move on. So, onward we went, even if it meant giving up my wonderful position in the community. Mostly, I was done, having enjoyed a great community position and lots of travel. Having arrived at this new place of unsettling in our marriage. I was missing America and my family and my freedom, plain and simple.

As simple as it was, I missed going to a store for things I had grown up with. I missed the freedoms we take for granted in America. My daughter, a few years old now, had never been to a mall. (There are worst things, right? But, at the time, I was frustrated by the limited shopping and the constant frustration to meet some of our needs). I remember when we went home for Christmas one year when she was about five. We went into a department store where little girl dresses hung. It was the first time at five years old that she had expressed any interest in fashion.

"Mommy, mommy, I want that one! Oh, look at that! Oh, I love zebra, oh I love the fur on the trim!" She wanted to buy it all; I had to calm her down. After all, there still was a budget. We loved going to the mall that Christmas. And that's when I realized she had never had a similar shopping experience in Germany. It is a silly thing, but I grew up with malls on every corner in South Florida. It's where you went when you outgrew your clothes or when you wanted to decorate your house or simply to spend time walking around for entertainment. In Germany, there were no malls in our area.

More important than any material item we couldn't find, we were missing family terribly. We packed up all of our baggage and our children and we travelled home on the eight hour flight for the holidays. It was a great effort. It was expensive and definitely inconvenient. We would pack and unpack bags, live out of suitcases and cram the entire family into one room at one of our family's homes. We had nowhere to sleep when we arrived and never enough money to get hotel rooms – we would have needed two. We were looking forward to moving home to stay to avoid the stress of these types of visits. It was simply time to go home.

But the Army is never on your time table, they have a mission and a plan all their own and often, we're the last ones to find out what that is, making it all the more stressful and nearly impossible to map out your life in advance. Our lives remained in flux with little information and an uncertainty of what was to come next. It's part of the being in the military. It was our way of life. And we had to learn to adjust.

CHAPTER SEVEN

CALLING THE TROOPS–A FAMILY INVADED BY STRESS

S tress has a funny way of showing itself, but in the soldier, it eventually led to mounting anger and a lot of loud expression of that anger. I remember one time closing myself in the bathroom just rocking myself back and forth, tears streaming down my face, praying for miracles; praying that he would just clam up and go away and stop barking at me. The stress had already percolated and the tea pot had already steamed over.

He often was yelling at the children. We lived in small quarters in Ansbach, a three bedroom flat. It was three bedrooms and a broom closet that would soon become my mother's visiting quarters. Often times the kids would be wrestling around or running up and down the hallway and something would crash on the floor and their daddy would encounter it and he would simply explode greater than the magnitude of the offense. I would come over with towels to mop up the damage and say, "They are only children; they're only playing. We're stuck inside because it's snowing outside, we have to make allowances for that." The weather was certainly an obstacle. Snow, snow and more snow and longer winter seasons, with only a brief summer reprieve. This was quite difficult for a South Florida girl and certainly for three growing children wanting only to be outside at the playground.

And the anger like that just seemed to mount all of the time. There was always stress or tension in the house. I was praying for miracles before we had even left the first duty station. I remember going to the church and openly asking for prayer. I was hoping that we would find a way to reach him, but his anger, forced down as depression soon started percolating up and outward as constant verbal explosion. We were constantly living with yelling and frustration, bickering and unrest and me trying to come to the rescue to soothe sad spirits.

Yet, we had to live life amidst this chaos, ignore the obstacles and the tension; we had to keep making goals, achievements and striving toward the victories– and there were some. I soon took a position about three months after the move to our new duty station. It was one of the few positions open on post. I was disappointed after my fantastic leadership position in Fulda, to not find employment in Ansbach right away.

After about three months, I became an admissions counselor for City Colleges of Chicago. And I also volunteered in the community, hoping to find my way into a different open position. I volunteered to put on a food event as a demonstrator for Cinco de Mayo for Army Community Services. I put together this food program to make guacamole and tortilla chicken and fresh salsa and a fiesta of Mexican food for a small group of wives.

It was to my benefit to volunteer then, because the hiring authority for the human relations department was present and after seeing my demonstration, said, "We want you on our team."

There wasn't an open position at the time, but they had appropriations for a special projects officer that they could put me in until a new position was funded in the new fiscal year. While it wasn't quite marketing and journalism, I would become an expert in customer service, marketing events and become part of the board of the moral welfare and recreation center and key leadership for the community. I was working for the DCA, Director of Community Affairs and the military lieutenant community in special projects.

The new position seemed to offer relief in many ways. I settled down because I had a place I fit and a position with a paycheck. My husband was focused on his transition and seemed pretty happy with his unit and his duties. It seemed like Ansbach would be a good fit for us and then the deployments and separations began to increase.

I decided at that time that it was a perfect time to earn my master's degree. The military offered educational programs at satellite offices for military soldiers and their families. They would bring in professors from well-known universities and offer programs. The University of Oklahoma was offering a Master's in Human Relations degree at Wurzburg, Germany and I decided, in spite of the ninety mile commute (each way), I would commit to the 18 month program to earn my master's degree.

I was working full time in the community, supporting the lieutenant colonel in his mission of excellence and offering quality programs to soldiers and their family members. My husband was deployed often during this time and I had three children at home, but I knew education was important and this goal had been important to me for a long time; now was a good time as any. As a military spouse, I was determined to keep moving forward in life, because if not, the military and its transitions and demands and missions and disruptions, would hold me back.

I really had a dream of getting an MBA but I didn't have enough confidence in my math skills. Life and people had shown up along the way to make me feel it was out of my reach.

I knew that I could likely never be able to get through all of the math required of an MBA program, so when I saw the MHR program and only a few math classes, I signed up right away, determined to succeed.

I signed up with another military spouse, a mutual friend, and she and I carpooled to classes. It was worth the drive and our friendship blossomed as we struggled through and encouraged one another through one exam after another. Often times during this eighteen month program my husband was deployed and I had to manage homework after a long day of work, as well as household chores at night, around school attendance and taking care of the kids. It was a very demanding time, but I really grew and found it enriching. My boss at work took an active interest in my education and became my mentor and my sponsor when it was time to do my internship. She was very supportive and encouraging.

Just two flights of stairs above us, a friend offered home daycare and became a great support as I took this on while my soldier was deployed. When I had to leave for work at seven o'clock in the morning, I could walk upstairs and there she was to lovingly care for my children.

Often times she would keep them late at night when I had to go to class and wouldn't get home until 11 p.m. It's sad that with the transition of the military we lose track of so many folks who showed up to help and love us through our lives and raising our children. Thank you to all of you, even our paths no longer count, your support and care made such a difference in the lives of my children and in mine. Like my mother, without whose help I likely would never had been able to work, travel so much or finish up my degree requirements. My mother came for a full semester to watch the kids while I balanced all the demands. Basically, you had to learn to be a good juggler to be a military wife, but support of neighbors, care givers, employers and moms made the job a lot more manageable.

Happily, I received my Master's in Human Relations degree in spite of my life's demands and the math. It turns out, I had more skill than I realized. I nailed statistics and much to my surprise, the professor used my exam as a class example stating it was perfect.

That success and public confirmation gave me confidence to know that one day I would pursue my MBA without fear. Sadly, after having worked so hard, that would be the only public recognition I would get. Another impact of being a military spouse is that I couldn't attend my hard-earned graduation ceremony. I always wondered why people would work so hard for something so big and not show up – now I knew first hand. The pomp and circumstance was scheduled for July and the Army released us to PCS back to the states at the end of May. I would miss the ceremony by six weeks and in that time there would be a lot of pomp and more cir-cumstance to come.

CHAPTER EIGHT

MICKEY AND MINNIE'S DEMISE

The stress in our marriage was mounting and I tried many things to address it. I had a lot of information to pull from as I was studying human relations and taking marriage and therapy counseling, grief and loss counseling in my master's program during this time, about the time the pressure was really gaining momentum. I was getting a lot of good information and I thought it would be very helpful for us to reflect on some of what I was learning.

My husband would have no part in this; he didn't want to be told there was something wrong with our marriage and certainly not with any of his behaviors. He just knew he was unhappy. His anger mounted as did his frustration and he projected it onto the kids. He was not very engaged with us and I would often take them outside to play just so they would not sit watching reruns of Star Wars or Star Trek, his favorite things.

I finally left him a note during my class one night. I told him it was time to step up because I was growing weak and was not going to put up with it anymore. It was time to engage with the children and support me, to be there to pick them up after work if he could and to help me out at home more.

I was at my limit, going to school, working and being a mother while he was away being G.I. Joe. When I came home from a full day of Saturday class, he had paid attention and did something very special. He got the kids involved, too. From counter to counter, the entire kitchen was covered with flour, pots, pans and dishes, but he sat me down as soon as I got home and closed the kitchen doors so I couldn't focus on the mess and presented me with a beautiful homemade ravioli meal, hand cooked, with candles on the table and a tasty variety of foods.

The kids were so proud of him and I was so proud to know that he had finally responded–he had heard me! I was so certain that that would be the breakthrough we needed. I appreciated it so deeply. In fact, right after that, I set up for us to go to a week of cooking school in Italy, for his birthday a few weeks away.

But after that and in between, nothing changed. He was angry, we were frustrated, it was stressful, he was taking it out on the kids and me; there was constant anger and he was not engaging in positive ways.

I was feeling like I was a single mother in my own home. I needed answers. I went to the church and I prayed out loud to those who had just asked for prayer intentions. I prayed that others would pray for our marriage and that there would be an encounter weekend at our church. I can't believe I did that in such a public way, but that's what church is for. They did offer a marriage retreat and I asked if he would go, but he refused.

So instead, I created our own encounter using the tools from my master's degree class, hoping that when we were away at cooking school we could have private encounter. But there really wasn't a god time to bring it up and I was awkward and intimidated and he didn't want to have anything to do with it anyway. It was a failed attempt.

But the trip was a great success, one of our best together while overseas. It was always more peaceful when we travelled. We could pretend our problems didn't exist and the stress and constant activity and confusion of having five kids around and constantly at bay wasn't there to wear him down. We were still somewhat at odds with one another, but we were having a fabulous time just enjoying the beauty of Cinque Terra and Italy and learning to cook Italian food from Italian cooks; it was as if everything was perfect. But then we headed home and it was immediately time for another deployment and the days leading up to it were very tenuous and stressful.

This time he would deploy to Cyprus. I was growing angry and resentful from the load of taking care of the children mostly alone and working on the other post, a short, but bothersome drive from home. I had so much on my plate and he was never there to help me and he was deploying yet again. And to rub salt in the wound, he was actually enjoying this deployment on the shores of Cyprus. He earned a diving certification and frequently had free time to explore the area; he was actually having fun and it made it even worse for me.

He would tell me about it because he was excited to share, but I heard it differently. I heard it that he was having fun and I was stuck in the house with all of the problems and all of the laundry.–the laundry I had to carry down three flights to the basement to get to the military-issued washing machines. It was not fair that I had to go outside to scrape the snow and ice from the car to get to work while he was having fun in a sunny destination. The military was his choice, but it had become my life and I resented it more and more.

He would go into town and enjoy the local foods and fun – I don't blame him, really, but he made friends with a hotel owner and the environment got a little too cozy for my comfort. They would have gatherings for the soldiers for R & R (rest and relaxation), and when I learned of this, I was jealous. I worked hard, took care of our kids, went to school and had no social reprieve. After his return, I saw a picture with him in it and six or eight men and women and he had his arm draped around another gal across her shoulder. Of course, she was likely just a gal that was there or maybe even partnered with somebody else–he swore there was no intention.

But from my perspective, I was lonely and it was hard to buy this story that he had slept in the restaurant owner's hotel upstairs after the party. He was a married man miles away from his wife. How could I trust that there wasn't something going on when I knew of so many soldiers that had been deployed to Korea, a year unaccompanied and they had fallen prey to women available overseas that had affected their marriages as well as cost them their marriages? This was the plight of so many married soldiers during extended deployments.

How could I trust that he was over there just relaxing and unwinding at a nice event where both men and women gathered? I wasn't there. It was hurtful and he was deployed yet again and I was frustrated with the whole Army situation.

Upon his return, I would have some very exciting news to share, or so I thought. He was home for a very short time before having to go to training and I asked him to sit on the couch with me and I announced to him that baby number four was on his way. I don't know what happened at that time. I couldn't begin to explain the sadness in his heart. For whatever reason, he didn't talk to me for a solid week. He just silently stewed. Mostly I was at work or school, but when I was home, there was silence. It was very confusing. We had both agreed to have ten children, we were married and we both created this baby – was it something more? In his heart of hearts, maybe he thought I had had this baby with somebody while he was deployed. The deployments and separation were a bed for confusion and doubt on both sides.

I promise to this day, I was a faithful wife. I want to believe in my heart of hearts he was a faithful spouse. But deployments are not healthy ways to build strong marriages. Separations in the military uniquely create a lot of stress and hardship on the individuals left to face the challenges at home, with a heavy load, little information and battling fear of the unknown every day.

The soldiers are left to face the mission in front of them, of fighting a war on little sleep with cold meals, with MREs out of a package, lots of stress, lots of sadness and great bitterness forms during those periods. Who is to say when he came back where he was emotionally?

Maybe he was ready to separate, having just enjoyed the freedom of a relaxing deployment with no family stress? Maybe he was ready to start enjoying dinners with men and women, adults and friendships where babies didn't fit in. Maybe his anger had nothing to do with the baby on the way or with me; maybe he wanted more for us and was frustrated by the limitation the Army placed on us. Rather than going on and asking why, I can only tell you my truth: he did not speak to me for a week after I told him baby four was on the way.

During this deployment my world was being rocked already as I would discover Mickey and Minnie's demise. Anytime a relationship was broken, it hurt me to my core, because as a child I knew the pain of broken marriages. My family was broken when I was four. I vowed when I was a little girl to never give up, to keep my children from the pain of having to choose one parent or the other. When I was a child, I had to push through my heartache every time I had to decide, did I want to go to my mother's or my father's – I wanted to be with them both.

When I had to decide whose home I wanted to spend Christmas in and where I would live; I shed tears until I was twelve, thirteen even fourteen. I dreamed a Cinderella dream as little girls do, that my parents would get back together. I vowed then that I would never, ever get a divorce. I vowed then that I would never, ever let my children come from a broken home.

So when families were broken, it resonated with me because I understood the pain. This one week, during that deployment, I was home sick from work. I was very sick and had to take off work. I lay on my couch with a fever, fighting the flu as my children played and entertained themselves around the living room within my sight. There was no one to help me -no mother nearby, no aunt nearby, no nanny in my home–there was just me. Many military wives can relate to my plight.

My military husband was deployed on a training exercise in Cyprus and I was solo parenting – sick or not, kids need caring for, food needs cooking and life keeps going. I was flat out on that couch during that time when I got the call that my brother was getting a divorce. I always thought of him and his wife as Mickey and Minnie. Mickey and Minnie can't part ways. How could that be? They lived in Orlando; they lived near Disney World, in fact, he worked for Disney World . They had come to Germany to celebrate a second honeymoon a previous year–they were who we looked up to for role model families. They were always laughing–they were happy in my eyes. How could Mickey and Minnie divorce? It set in the seed of doubt like no other.

I knew that if they could get a divorce, then no one was safe, my husband and I were also vulnerable to such demise. As I lay there on the couch full of fever and contemplating this sadness, I realized that nothing was sacred or permanent or for certain–that anything could happen.

That maybe my husband could find himself in a weak moment during deployment or that maybe he would return and the seed of sadness really was that he didn't love me anymore or didn't want the burden or responsibility that comes from a big family anymore. It really was the beginning.

Maybe we weren't meant to be married forever and ever. Maybe that thinking was just part of my fever and who knows how it would pan out but right then, it rocked my world real hard.

CHAPTER NINE

IN NEED OF A FAIRY GODMOTHER

The world is big and there were many international destinations to be encountered and conquered. I had a list going; I always knew where was I was going to travel to next and in my free time I planned the next trip to ensure I would be prepared and wouldn't miss a single opportunity.

It didn't matter if the money was budgeted but not yet available, it didn't matter if I didn't know which weekend on the calendar was going to fit, but I dreamt. I had the calendar in front of me and travel books in arms all of the time. Sooner or later my plans and my free time and funding would all line up and off I'd go.

Fodor's and Frommer's were my bedside reading. I would constantly ask friends, "Where would you go? Where did you go? What have you seen? What did you love the most?" I would often go to the military travel center, SATO, and the military travel office, ITT. They offered ongoing day trips for soldiers and their family members. They had the travel plan down pat. Get on a bus at six o'clock in the morning, go to another country and be back by midnight, having seen all the major sights and tasted some great local foods. It was reasonably priced and everything you needed to shop and drop, taste, see and experience.

I signed up for many of them, baby belly and all. Around my work schedule I would find ways to be available in small chunks of time to see other countries. I remember one particular day trip, everyone was taken care of from child care to work routines and I headed to shop in Czechoslovakia.

I carried my own handles for the shopping bags that would soon be laden with crystal. We visited so many crystal shops that day. I found many treasures for our home and already had dreams for some of the pieces when we would return home stateside. My pregnant belly caused lots of stares as I walked like a duckling waddling down the sidewalk with all of these other fellow travelers. I was determined to take it all in, pregnant or not, and I enjoyed the simplicity of day tripping with a group.

I wouldn't have done it any other way. Traveling with a pregnant baby belly, traveling with a baby in a backpack, six months old, traveling with our family with strollers and children, whatever the circumstance of the time, nothing was holding us back from seeing it all. Travel was my passion and my greatest pleasure after a simple day at home with the kids. We were going to see and experiences all that the military was offering us, and in the end, I did my best to rack up the passport stamps. But then came baby number four and I was sick as a dog and still working and the soldier was deployed, so I slowed down to a crawl, but never fully stopping.

I was seasick twenty four hours a day without reprieve for nine months, except maybe one day for no explainable reason. It was like being on a ship with seasickness–twenty four hours a day. My husband was deployed from January to May that time and I was pregnant with our fourth child. In addition to motherhood, my work was in full swing and we were leading the process for competing in Army Communities of Excellence, a Malcolm Baldridge program. There was a lengthy application process over about 8 months time and weekly meetings and programs I designed to support the application process. The hard work paid off for our team and the community was recognized for the large community win, which yielded incentive money for community improvements and important recognition. There were four of us hand-selected to represent the community as ambassadors and to go to the Pentagon in Washington D.C. to receive the award.

Here I was being spotlighted for the greatest honor of my career and my husband was deployed. I needed family nearby to care for my three children so I could participate. The sweet care giver who provided daily in-home daycare agreed to watch the children for a week so that I could travel back to the United States, with my pregnant belly and all. What a gift she offered me. It was a wonderful honor to go to the Pentagon and receive this award.

The deployment ended right after I returned. I went back to work after our award trip, but my heart wasn't really in it anymore. Although we had won this great award, I had finally reached my peak; I was tired as a parent. I was constantly sick and tired of being a single parent and I knew it was time to do something. There was another impending separation due to training and I knew I had reached my limit, so I took a leave of absence, packed up the kids and headed to the states to finish up my pregnancy, deliver the baby stateside and hopefully find some relief in family. I was in my last trimester and my husband was finishing up training at Fort Rucker, Alabama. For six weeks we lived out of a hotel and swam in the pool for entertainment. I went to visit family and then settle in with his folks in their home in Jacksonville, Florida, until he was finished with his program, closer to the baby's delivery.

Was this a good choice or not? My kids had to be put into a year round school because that was the school system that was available to them there.

The school wasn't very welcoming and the schedule was very upsetting. My kindergartener who had just started had a very rigorous academic curriculum to follow. He had to be telling stories and writing them on the computer in full sentences by the end of his first week of kindergarten.

It was quite a shock, he is bright and was able to achieve this, but there was no time to adjust. My older son had quite a struggle; his teacher didn't really seem to put any extra energy into him because she knew he would only be there temporarily. He struggled every day and some of the events of the day were very disheartening. It wasn't a very positive situation. It broke my heart, but I knew it was temporary and tried to just get him through.

At home, the elderly grandmother who lived in the house and I would cook the meals and spend time together bonding. At the end of the day, we cooked for thirteen people every night. I wasn't getting much rest between being a mother to the three kids and being sick twenty four hours a day.

My husband was at yet another school another state away and as Murphy's military wives' law would have it, all three children would come down with chickenpox exactly one month before my due date. Sibling love.

There I was having to care for these three children while in my last month of pregnancy. My mother couldn't come and help me because she had never been exposed to chickenpox and my mother in law was preparing for a son's wedding and they all went to North Carolina the week of my due date, leaving me home with one grandma and a pregnant belly. (My husband went with my blessing. I figured the baby would wait and family weddings wouldn't). After three weeks of chickenpox, I was happy to stay home and let them go to the wedding so I could rest.

Not so much rest as I would have liked as my sciatic was acting up during this pregnancy and I had to get in and out of bed with a cane. I would make it through the wedding weekend and deliver a few days later. I had prayed for an easy delivery and God was gracious to answer my prayers. My husband returned home from his military training and the wedding and was on leave as we waited for the baby to come. We went grocery shopping for the entire family at the commissary as my labor pains started that morning. When I got home, I decided to mention their growing intensity and said, "I think it's time to go; we should hurry to unpack the groceries." By the time we got the hospital, he had nearly arrived. He was born in less than thirty two minutes after our arrival.

I had prayed for an easy delivery and my prayers had been answered. It was a civilian hospital so the experience was different from the births in the military hospital, but not much. It was an especially crowded day and they originally wanted me to give birth in the hallway on a gurney when I arrived. When I protested, they found an empty operating room and pushed me inside just about the time it was to deliver. It happened so quickly.

Within one week after the baby was born, my husband was off again. He had to go back to training at Fort Rucker, Alabama and there we remained in waiting in Jacksonville, Florida. I was anxious to show my newborn baby off to my mother, my uncle and my siblings in South Florida. It was only five hours away and I assumed I could certainly do such an easy trip.

I loaded up my three children, the new baby and myself in the van and we drove down south the five hours to my Uncle's house. However, I'm not sure what I was thinking. It is assumed we know that we shouldn't be in the car driving five hours by ourselves on an interstate with toddlers that have to go to the bathroom and need snacks and cry and need naps at different times and I was one lone, weepy, easily overwhelmed, five days post-partum momma. What was I thinking?

By the time I got to my uncle's in North Palm Beach I was a mess and I'm sure I was crying. This is part of being a military spouse. If you want it done you have to do it yourself. But sometimes, it would be easier having a spouse to help along the way!

After enjoying a week of rest with my family and showing off my baby and his siblings, I turned around and drove back to Jacksonville where I was left to single handedly pack our entire family's belongings into duffle bags, preparing to go back overseas where I would go back to work and we would finish up our tour of duty before our final PCS back to the states.

I was on the floor of this large master bedroom suite at our in-laws home with children sword fighting and the baby crying, pulling down all of the gifts I had just gotten at my baby shower off the shelf, all of the toddler papers from their various schools, the school folders, clothes pile after clothes pile, duffle bag after duffle and suitcase after suitcase trying to fill them, and yet,

I couldn't seem to get it all to fit. It wouldn't fit and it wouldn't end and the baby was crying and wanting attention and I was trying not to.

My mother-in-law finally came upstairs and took one look at my dilemma and said, "I feel so bad for you." She went right to the Army supply store and bought a couple tremendous duffle bags like the kind a soldier would use when he deployed and she offered them to me as a gesture of support.

She provided three or four of these and I filled them up by stuffing all of our belongings into them. It was the best gift she ever gave me, even though I was left to pack them myself, at least she had showed me that her heart was with me. Trying to get out of the country was another story. I had to return ahead of my soldier husband because I had to get back to work and he was still in training.

My husband wasn't there to send us off and we were going to fly out of Charleston, South Carolina according to military orders. We were taking a military flight because of all of the children and the expense of flying. We rented a car and drove there and my brother in law was so gracious to drive down from North Carolina and meet me there just so that he could load and unload the bags for me because the load was so overwhelming. That was very helpful gesture, but it didn't simplify our send off. As we were checking in our big crew and our multiple bags, I found out that my newborn baby was not free to fly. The baby and I were only five weeks postpartum.

Who knew there was a rule that you cannot travel overseas unless you have had a final medical check prior to six weeks postpartum. There I was standing in the middle of this military terminal with three kids, a new baby, no husband and five weeks postpartum – you can only imagine. I felt so helpless.

A total stranger came to our rescue. A nearby passenger heard of our plight and just happened to be a military medical doctor. He agreed to give me a verbal exam so that the baby and I could be released. Thank fully, I had a very normal and healthy delivery and a verbal exam was sufficient to clear us.

It was very gracious of him and we were very lucky to get that close to losing our seats home. My brother-in-law had the big task of getting our car seats and duffle bags for three children, a newborn, and myself with over six months' worth of stuff, checked in so we could take off for our international flight home.

We arrived safely and somehow settled in just in time for the holiday commotion. The baby played Jesus in the Christmas nativity at our post chapel. It was a perfect gift for our return, his first Christmas and holi-days without family.

I reluctantly went back to work, but it wouldn't be for long, soon after returning to work, we found out that we were going to return to the United States for our next tour of duty by the end of May. I was happy we were finally going home. It was going to be a career transition I wasn't ready for, but I knew it was time. I prepared for our move after five and a half years overseas. I was responsible for all of the packing and labeling of our belongings and separating it into hold baggage, advance cargo and household goods we could live without for at least six weeks on the other end of receiving.

We had been dreaming of building our own home when we returned to the states. I could picture the cars we would drive and I could picture us getting out of this funk that we had fallen into in Germany. Germany had been great for us and we traveled to many places, but we had stayed beyond our limits and the duration was taking its toll. I was anxious to get back to the States.

I was missing the States, I was missing malls–I was an American through and through. I wanted to live off the military kaserne, but still be proud of serving. I wanted to have a life without restrictions, with more freedoms. I wanted to raise my children in my own country, in our communities and what was familiar and I was just anxious to get back even though I held Germany and her people in high esteem and the memories dear and deep in my heart.

When we got back, there was no joy to greet us, tragedy would be waiting around the corner. there was more sadness, more loss and greater hardship. This time it had nothing to do with the military and it was just by luck we were back on home soil. My family was all gathering the last weekend in May at my brother's house in Orlando, celebrating family birthdays and our coming back to the states when we got the phone call that my sister's son was tragically killed in a motorcycle accident.

We had already lost family children to drowning–not once, but twice. And here would be a third loss for our family of one of our young ones. It was not the way I envisioned our welcome home back to the States; our hearts ached from the news. The first week was a week of funerals, where we drove to Louisiana and said goodbye to our most precious Christopher Matthew, with his blonde ringlets and his beautiful smile and the freckles across the bridge of his nose.

I used to sing *The Itsy Bitsy Spider* song to him when he was a toddler. I used to carry him on my hip and help raise him when he was a baby so full of joy. I lived with my sister when I was a junior and senior in high school and helped her to raise this son just after she went through a divorce. It was such sadness and it didn't help our transition at all.

After the news, we all flew to Louisiana for the services and then drove to Texas where my sister lived for the funeral services. It was a long, sad week and my husband had to report to training in Alabama. I had my daughter and baby as I travelled to Texas. When we were done, we were going to a new tour of duty located in Fort Eustis, Virginia.

When we arrived ahead of our soldier who was still in training, there were no quarters immediately available. My mother came along to help with the kids and my move and we waited it out in on-post Space A accommodations. You show up early in the name, put your name on a list and based on rank and availability you are assigned a room. There was a lot of show up and wait around and see, but we got in that night to rest as we waited to receive our quarters the next day.

CHAPTER TEN

CAREERS, QUARTERS AND SCHOOLS: THE NEVER ENDING SEARCH

W hen we got to Fort Eustis, we soon learned we would be living in on-base housing. It would be a cinder block, two story townhome attached to another house with little yard and dilapidated interior; not my idea of the custom home I dreamed about. There would be no newness for us and endless stories of having to overcome obstacles.

When I arrived the house was in unacceptable conditions. My mother and I gingerly inspected the quarters. The bathtub should have been quarantined–it was stripped of all of its finish. The kitchen floor was so marred and filthy, I would later insist my husband had to retile it before I would allow the children to walk on it. To make matters worse, intruders had broken in during the night and used the home for their escapades; it left a sick feeling in my stomach. My husband was at his training assignment the day my mother and I received our household goods. It was a lot of work juggling babies and toddlers, boxes and workers in the hot summer sun.

To me, it was a six month prison sentence where we lived from ceiling to floor, with boxes stacked tightly in the dining room because the quarters were not big enough for our household goods. We knew it would be temporary; I did what I could to make it live-able. I created a space for the kids to play and a place for us to be comfortable. The kids would play soccer in the field in front of our home and we would have to make it work, but to me it was miserable and barely tolerable.

It was not long after we moved in that I quickly began our search for a new house off-post. Military housing terms stated that even though we were completely dissatisfied on post and even though our children were not able to attend school on post due to space limitations, we had to stay in quarters to fulfill a six month contract.

The kids began private school in the Catholic school there, at our Lady of Mt. Carmel, and I began the commute: twenty minutes each day, each way, three times a day because the younger grade got out two hours earlier than the older grades. I was constantly in the car and it certainly added to the stress of our family. I soon found the house of our dreams about twenty minutes away. It was very close to the church and the school, which was very important to me and would finally ease my burden.

There we were at Fort Eustis, Virginia, new arrivals and I was out of work again, as a military spouse, looking to start again as my husband reported for duty at his assigned station. I spent much of my free time – as if there was any–on the computer, searching Monster. com and other career search engines for open positions. I spent hours upon hours filling out applications. I tried to get creative at this point.

I remember once trying to rely on my Tupperware experience as a unit manager and I sent my resume in a Freezer Mate Container to the Tupperware headquarters saying, "Don't put my resume in the deep freeze, call me for work!" I tried anything that was creative, desperate for an opportunity. I went to the museum downtown because they were looking for a director of communications and thought it would be a direct fit for my marketing services overseas. I did a marketing survey and created a marketing proposal for them pitching what I

164

would do if I were to get the position. I presented them with lots of good ideas for facility improvement and customer experience enhancement.

They could tell by my resume that I was not there for the long haul; they knew I was a military spouse and I didn't get that position either. It was through a personal connection that I was able to get a short- term position in the training department of a national headquarters as a technical writer. But how uncomfortable, the position and environment was not a good fit for me and I was unhappy in that position.

I was in a dark cubicle all day long, for eight hours a day with very little interaction from my peers, and once more I shared the office with a co-worker who insisted that the lights be out during the week day and we work off the computer monitor's light. It was a dark and depressing position. But when you can't find work and you are a military spouse, you take what you can and try to make it work.

Finally, I was able to be in off-quarters housing and I could say goodbye to the long and repetitive daily commute to school and my children had the privilege of going to Catholic school for two years, which had always been a dream of mine. They were there, but it's not to say it was easy; it was such a challenge with the carpool situation before we moved and the nuns didn't offer much understanding or flexibility for our personal demands or family history. I remember one time sitting around the conference table having a discussion about my oldest son's academic progress and telling her about the stresses in our family, how much we had to manage and how inconvenient it was for the traveling and the financial commitment and so on.

We talked about my son's inattentiveness, his inability to sit still and his difficulty in keeping up with the class. As I began to talk about how our family life and military life had impacted his studies, she rolled her eyes at my 'excuses'. I remember saying, "Nobody would do what I do. It is such a challenge to be a military spouse with multiple children, moving time and again, living with military quarters that are unacceptable and just trying to make life work."

She rolled her eyes in such a disapproving way and non-affirming way, but it was a pivotal moment for me. As I reflected upon that day after day, I realized, yes, while my life was challenging, while the military put us in a unique situation, I was still so very blessed to have so many beautiful children, healthy and well and the opportunity of a great education in front of us. At this time our family was still intact, even if we were presenting cracks in our financial and emotional foundations. I didn't convey to her the level of stress in our home or after church every Sunday, there wasn't so much peace in our family car. I was reflecting on the front pew family that we were and how the steam poured out on the drive all the way home and not a word of Father's homily seemed to diffuse the stress or heal the wounds our hectic military life had created. Instead, I tried to reframe my thinking and get out of myself and realize it could always be worse. I just had to try harder to see the sunny side of life.

Chapter Eleven

The Fairytale Ends

We were front row Catholics at Our Lady of Mt. Carmel. The family would get up with mixed resistance, amidst shouting and fussing and would get dressed in our Sunday best and take our seats in the very front row. We would listen to Monsignor and his very moving and powerful homily. We knew many in the parish from the Catholic school and our Catholic community of friends and we looked forward to connecting every Sunday.

It was a fulfilling and rewarding time every Sunday morning, but as soon as we would get in the car, his anger would start. He would be frustrated over the children, the traffic or something I said. He would be raging at the cars or irritated about the commotion in the car while we made our 20 minute drive home. The anger was just bubbling within him and he poured it out, taking it out on all of us.

I tried to deflect the bullets by having a conversation with the children and ignoring his fury. "Did anyone learn anything today? What did you hear the priest say? What was something that made a difference to you? Let's talk about how that could impact our family and how we could make it work for us."

But he would continue to get agitated and irritated and before we ever made it home, we were all arguing and bickering and dissatisfied in that car. We had a new beautiful house to walk into, but the peace evaded us there, too. We thought it would be a great idea to have the priest come and bless the house. As the house was still being framed and the security system wires were being installed, the priest dropped by the house unexpectedly. I was not there so my husband greeted him.

He blessed each of the door frames and left a permanent mark on the wooden beams. My husband was a witness to this blessing of our home. Somehow I thought that was a wonderful idea: a blessed house would bring a blessed family and blessings to our home. Perhaps, I should have been present for the blessing, too, because a house divided will not stand, we were soon to learn. Somehow I believe it was the beginning of the spiritual warfare for our family – not that that act invited it, because we added plenty of fuel to the fire on our own, but the new house and the blessing seemed to be symbolic to the walk of warfare.

The neighborhood was a perfect new community to raise our children and bond with other young couples and connect. We had an awesome neighborhood and all moved in about the same time, due to the new construction and the rate of growth in the neighborhood.

The neighbors had children the same ages as ours and the couples were like-minded, though only one or two associated with the military, all working families, working for their family. We gathered often to socialize, share, encourage and help one another. Our bonds grew, friendships flourished and eventually, we would become the extended family for one another as most of ours were in far away states.

I was the self-proclaimed hostess of the neighborhood. We gathered on every occasion for Christmas parties to Easter egg hunts, usually 35- 50 neighbors, families and kids alike. Our house was the gathering place, because I was always the first to extend the invitation. I loved sharing hospitality and friendship with each one of my neighbors.

A highlight from one of our favorite gatherings was the Fourth of July parade where we all put on our patriotic styling and decorated the kid's wagons and strollers and paraded around our little neighborhood, which eventually grew into a larger development. The children eagerly got involved and decorated their bikes, too, and we paraded around the neighborhood blaring horns, laughing and cheering, blessed to be friends and neighbors and proud to be Americans.

We walked around and greeted the neighbors who participated and sometimes stopped on front lawns of those who didn't, but who cheered us on, too. After our morning parade, we would gather at one house or another and often have a chili cook-off or some other kind of typical American pot luck gathering. We had a wonderful neighborhood. Our kids had friends, they played in safety. We had friends, our life wasn't lonely. Our family seemed peaceful, happy and congenial.

But behind closed doors it was always another story. Inside of our home, there was always a lot of crankiness, fussing, anger and boiling rage. I was always trying to defuse it. I would try to deflect his anger, to encourage the children to do another activity to shift the atmosphere. I was stressed and under constant pressure, from raising five kids to refereeing the constant emotional fire and bending under the financial pressures of raising a large family with one military paycheck.

There was the obvious load of nine to thirteen loads of laundry every week. Every day there were chores at the rate of seven people a day, every day there were meals to be made at a rate of at least five a day, every day there were activities to taxi to and seeds to plant and gardens to tend and feelings to mend. It was a lot to manage because he rarely got involved and when he did, there was guaranteed conflict. He stayed mostly in retreat mode and I just lead the brigade.

Military hours were often not normal hours, but extended hours; he was often gone ten and twelve hours a days. If there was an impending event or a pending situation, he was on call or was called to work until the needs of that demand were met. I learned to organize and manage around that, but I didn't always accept that willingly. I welcome my big family, love the challenge, the spirits of each, the workload it carries with such a number. I love to cook and care and nurture and serve, what I'm expressing is that it is simply a large burden and more so when one parent bears most of the work load alone, while under financial and emotional stress.

The emotional stress was really the apple that upset the cart. It was not unusual for temper s to be going at full speed and we're trying to maneuver our way around the words and the anger and the doorbell would ring, one of our neighbors coming over to say hello or give us something and immediately we would all freeze, paralyzed in order to keep the truth of what was really going on hidden behind the door. He would open the door and become the mayor of the community; cheerful, welcoming and joyful, trying to keep his composure.

They would never have a clue about what was happening behind that door. The door would close and the argument and tension would resume. It is as if we lived two lives. At first, the pressure was just emotional stress and constant burden of running a big household in a big house, then the financial pressures increased and the weight of his constant absence and his eventual PCS to Fort Bragg, took its greatest toll and the volcano erupted to a new level, particularly following the Afghanistan deployment. He supported Operating Enduring Freedom, but it became Operation Enduring Hardship for us at home.

In his absence, our friends and our neighbor became our family. They helped support me when I needed someone to care for the children. While there weren't very many military families in our neighborhood, these friends could understand being away from their own extended families what it must be like and they substituted as our family and offer extra help.

The relief care they offered was exactly what I needed during his absence, but it didn't help as much when he was home. Mr. Arnold was a disengaged parent. During homework time, my oldest child would struggle with his homework and instead of being done in thirty to forty five minutes, he would be at his desk for three or four hours. He was often in tears trying to struggle through it. I would go in there periodically and give him guidance and try and offer him help. I often had to reach out to his teachers for help, but he struggled, anyway. I am sure it was from all of the transitions we went through, through the many schools he had to encounter. He had been to the military school in Ansbach and then to the year round school in Florida, and here we were, at another school in Virginia.

I remember him crying through his glasses, his daddy barreling down the hallway bellowing at him, "Do your homework! You are going to end up in prison if you do not do your homework! Why does it take you so long? I don't understand!" After that Kyle would be shaking and crying; he so much wanted to be successful, but either not having the tools or consistency in his early academic years combined with the constant stress of the house, placed him at a disadvantage for success. His Daddy's bellowing didn't improve the situation.

At bedtime, I often sat with the children and read books. A few times at bedtime, I would say, "Go read the children a book." And he would say, "Eh, they'll be fine," as he sat in his recliner and watched the television. Every night the children and I would retreat in their bedroom and I would read them bedtime stories. We finished novels like Robin Hood and Robinson Crusoe and every night I would tuck each one in with prayers and an individual Disney story, so each one had one on one time with me.

I would sing them the songs that I had made up for them. In my heart, I yearned for their father to get involved, for him to connect with them on another level. Instead, he retreated further into his own world; into his own anger and depression. Another particularly sad night was family game night. Every Friday night I would rent movies and eat pizza or make something simple for Family Night. We would often play games around the kitchen table.

Our room was divided by a little railing and he would sit in the living room watching TV with the remote control in his lap and the children and I would be around the family room table playing games like Monopoly, Yahtzee and Clue. One time I even had a cake made to celebrate our family. I wrote in bakery gel pen: It's Family Game Night, Let the fun begin! Let the good times roll.

We begged him to come over and join us, "Please come play with us – just one game? You are missing out!" And he said, "No. Games are for kids. I would rather sit here and watch." We played anyway and tried to be a little quieter so he could watch TV, but we weren't very good at the quiet part.

It was one example of how he was a disengaged parent. He was a hero to everyone–everyone else always seemed to get his best. He was a hero in his children's eyes; not to mislead you. But he wasn't good at engaging or taking leadership or being there when we really needed him. For example, the Hurricane in 2003; instead of being home to protect us, he volunteered to stay on post to help out.

Yes, he was a big help and he made a difference; there was a car that flooded and he helped the owner and he went and rescued people who were knee high in water and about to be in serious trouble. Yes, he was a hero at work. But he left me and five children underneath a dining room table, as the lighting took off and the rain came down. We were there with our flashlight, the children trembling with uncertainty and me to calm them, sing songs to them, tell them stories to distract them, all the time wondering if the hurricane would pass, would the walls cave in?

It would have been such a help, such a soothing encouragement to have my husband there. But he did what soldiers do during times of stress. He went out into the battlefield, he went into search and rescue mode from his Coast Guard days. He went to take care of everyone else not realizing that in that heroism, he wasn't taking care of those who mattered most.

That time is when the tree fell into our neighbor's home and I was left to manage it and figure out how to help and reach out. I am sure there were also roots of bitterness and anger within each of us from these missed events.

The children were angry their daddy was not home. I was angry that I had to watch my children's hearts break as my husband was unavailable, AWOL, or just plain steaming with woundedness. I was frustrated and resentful that I was home most of the time taking care of the laundry, the chores and the management of these five children of ours. I was resentful that I couldn't live near my family, hundreds of miles away in Florida, and enjoy life, food and family together. I was angry that we had no control over our lives, but were prisoners of our life.

There was always a lot of anger and unrest in our home. It stemmed from the military missions, I'm sure, but it went beyond that too, from the burden on the camel's back and one too many straws.

I knew we were really in trouble after our return from Germany and counseling was a likely solution, but in the military there is a stigma about this. I knew that medicine would help to make the problems manageable, but he refused to admit there was a problem, so there was no identified reason for medication. I know he recognized the problem, even though he stayed in firm denial, and I'm sure it was also because of the stigma. Any identified issue or medicine that might be deemed necessary could impair his military flying career.

I do believe that was one very big obstacle. He would never acknowledge that he could use help. As adults we know that it's not normal to constantly be yelling, raging and watching your children and the ones you love in tears. Certainly it isn't normal to function with so much constant and ongoing chaos and to pretend to the world that life is good. But where does one turn? How do you reach out for help? How do you stop the cycle? Putting my foot down, taking a stand only served to heat up the battle. What would our families think? What would the military think? What would we do with the labels that fly? How would we get the help we needed? When you're in the midst of this type of situation, it becomes so overwhelming, there are no easy answers and you don't know where to begin to find a solution. The choice becomes easier to live in denial. We had to learn to live with his anger, with the bitterness, with his frustration and our own and with his helplessness and with our brokenness.

Eventually, after enough eruptions, I found to the strength to make the call for help. I sat in the parking

lot of the counselor's office a very long while before getting the gumption to walk in, share my story and ask
for help.

CHAPTER TWELVE

PRISONERS OF WAR: A FAMILY GRIEVES THE LOSS

The counseling didn't really make a difference. When one doesn't acknowledge a dysfunction, there is nothing that can be addressed or resolved. After a few frustrating attempts , I pursued on my own for a few more visits, before relinquishing defeat and just in time for my competition to gear up and him to get a new assignment.

Instead of getting out of the military, as I had hoped, he got another assignment. I persisted month after month, "Do you think we could get out? Do you think this will be our last assignment? Will you please ask? Would you go to your commander and ask for retirement? I want to see it in writing." I never trusted he was following through.

180

We had agreed that at twenty years of service, we would get out of the military and move to Florida.

We would open a pizzeria or a bed and breakfast. Certainly, we had enough helping hands with all of our children. We would be near family–in fact, I would love nothing more than to live in the same neighborhood as my mother and my sisters and my brothers. I would love the kids to know their cousins and meet up for regular family meals – it was my idea of a big, Italian family.

Certainly, he would want the same things still, after all, it's what we had agreed to when we got married. But no, there would be no orders to get out; he would be reassigned to Fort Bragg, North Carolina for another tour – so much for a freedom pass.

I didn't take the news without protest. We were embedded in our community. I was a Girl Scout leader, the boys were in Boy Scouts, they loved their soccer coaches and their teachers at school–there was no moving us. So, I took a stand. I drew the line in the sand. I had finally had enough of all the moving and hardship and uprooting the kids and changing addresses.

"If you won't get out then I'll take a stand for our family. There will be no more military moves for us. I do not know what the answer is, really, I just prayed that you would get out. I have had enough of this life with prison walls, I have had enough of this anger that you carry hone to us and the effects on our children. I will no longer stand for this way of life. You can accept the orders, you can move to Fort Bragg, but we're going to stay behind in our home and in our community."

I made the choice to stay put for our family and he went ahead. Maybe the separation would help us, help let the steam out of the pot; either way, he would have to go ahead and figure it out. I was done and I was done begging him to retire from the Army that had stifled us and drained the life out of our marriage. He had to move ahead, he had no choice. No matter how much his heart was torn, he had to follow his military's orders. It was his mission, it was his passion, it's what he signed up for and it's what Uncle Sam required. So, he traveled to Fort Bragg and we stayed behind.

In doing so, we isolated ourselves from the military community we knew. We had no military connection, no military support groups, no morale and welfare facilities; we were pretty independent and immersed in the civilian community. I did have access to the commissary, but I was like a single woman living on an island, raising five children; there wasn't anyone wearing BDU's and no one waiting with me while their spouse was deployed. I just focused on raising the kids and getting through the days. He did travel back and forth on the weekends to stay connected and give us a little help with the chores that come from such a full house. He would mow the lawns on the weekend and reconnect with the kids, but, day by day, we were becoming more separated.

I knew that assignment would change us. I said it aloud and it was done. It was done, the dreams were dashed. We would no longer live happily ever after in a beautiful home under one roof. I would no longer be able to move to Florida and have the children grow up with their cousins. We would no longer open a pizzeria because this would change everything. And indeed it did.

While we waited out the tour, I assumed that we would soon be out of the military. The stress of raising five children on my own and manage our busy household on my own, was taking its toll. I slowly started to lose my grip and the stress mounted day after day. I lost my patience and often just ended up shouting into the abyss of my home. The stress of living in the military and the constancy of not knowing, wondering when we would be able to be free, when we could make our own choices deeply affected me. It affected my children. There was no information, nothing to calm us, give us hope or a vision for our future; the constant unknown became such a heavy burden to me and my husband or the military gave us no indication of reprieve – there was no release date in sight,

Even as this assignment seemed to be at a likely close, we were not going to get retirement orders, yet again, but deployment orders. Finally, he had received his orders for retirement, but they were quickly retracted as Operation Enduring Freedom got underway and he would soon be sent to Afghanistan instead of home.

He was going from department to department to get clearance signatures and had already turned in some of his military gear, preparing for his retirement transition when the government froze all retirement orders due to the mission on the horizon.

For a brief few days, we were relieved to know we would be released from duty and could finally move on toward retirement and our new future. I think he was scared to death because he didn't really have a vision for our future; retirement was not exactly what he wanted. I think he would have stayed in for another ten years had it not been for me constantly persisting. Although we had agreed at the beginning of our marriage to retire at 20 years, I think he changed his mind and could never bring himself to that conversation because he knew how much I wanted out.

I'm sure he wanted to honor us and be with his family, but he was torn. He had always only known the military. What else would he do? Who would he be? How would he make a living? Where would the security come from? How would he make ends meet? I'm sure it was very overwhelming from his perspective.

But we didn't have an opportunity at that juncture to work through those issues, because the mission comes first and he wasn't free to retire. As soon as the orders were rescinded, he was doing a reverse of his trail to reclaim the gear he had turned in and he went on a brief leave to come home and say goodbye to us.

He came home that weekend and we were preparing to say goodbye yet another time. Standing near the rose garden which he added to every Mother's Day for me, everything in our perimeter suddenly became very vivid and memorable. I knew it was a defining moment. The children were running around the yard as they often did and I had a knowing revelation as I looked at him against the arbor and the garden gate which he had built. As I sat there looking at him and smelling the fragrance of the nearby roses, I knew fully, he would not be the same when he returned. Things would change, they would be different.

What did that mean, I wondered? Would he come back as an amputee – something else? I don't know. I just knew at that moment in the garden, he would come back, but I knew he wouldn't be the same. And I was right because he came back seemingly intact on the outside, but his interior had cracked further.

The stress of military life was already presenting the stress fractures for a very long time.

For example, September 11, 2001 (9-11) was deeply impactful for everyone and because of our commitment to the military, we would have to manage through that experience by ourselves, not together as couples often do. Yet again, I was alone. Hurricanes, birthdays, baby deliveries and now terrorist attacks on our nation; I was left to my own emotions and to the care of my children. The children were at school, my daughter in her high-chair and he was at Fort Bragg, North Carolina, taking care of the demands of the country and his position. We were all in shock. He called me immediately and we watched it unfold on television. I just knew immediately it would resonate further, like a ripple effect and I was bracing for it. We were talking our way through it as we watched it play out on TV, but how I would have loved to have been held in those first few minutes. I would have preferred to have him to hug on, somebody to cling to – my husband to reassure me that the world wasn't ending that day even as we were watching it unfold. Instead, we were on the phone talking through it. Instead, I was watching it on the screen, processing it all and left with little to comfort me.

Everything stopped for the country after 9-11 and yet when you are a single mother, life goes on. That week, we grieved, we still went to school, we lit candles and went to vigil gatherings and we waited for our soldier to come home on the weekend. The gap for us widened again.

I was so deeply moved by those events. I have always held a dear affection for our country. When I was a teenager I won a national speech contest for my speech What's Right With America and when I competed in a Miss America preliminary, I performed a medley of Patriotic songs. I was the one to rally the neighbors for our annual Fourth of July parade and chili cook-off gathering. Maybe it was because my mother was raised during the war and passed on her affinity for the flag and our country. Maybe because my Daddy and brothers served, maybe because I was a Girl Scout, maybe because I was now a military spouse, supporting the mission of our country, but I always upheld our beautiful America and was deeply grieved by the events of 9-11. I wanted a channel to express that deep sorrow in a bigger way. I wanted to create a way for Americans to take do something, to turn that wrong into good, to rise from the ashes. I also wanted her to wake up, to remember our country and our values and what we stand for.

I was inspired to write a patriotic program called *Spirit of America Days*. I spent hours writing this program where we could pull together as a community to volunteer, to celebrate our great country, to decorate our houses and come together as communities where the spirit of America could be seen and our strength and resilience expressed and where people could lift one another up, neighbor helping neighbor.

It gave voice to all the energy and emotion and grief and strength to one possible response to our hurt from these events. It was a good outlet for my voice and I spent hours and evenings writing, developing it, creating packages and reaching out for public support from political leaders, but that would come in time and it didn't help the stress and the impact the accumulated stress had on my body.

All of the moves, the constant demands of single parenting, all of the wondering if he would ever get out of the military, all of the times he would come back and forth and the stress from those unending periods of transition, it finally revealed itself in my body. Something had infiltrated me by the following January. He was at Fort Bragg and I was alone taking care of the children and for five months I had such a deep pain in my bones, my joints, my body and my blood. There wasn't a specific diagnosis to determine what it was – maybe a transient virus, maybe non-descript effect of the unending stress.

I had an MRI, I went to doctors and still the stiffness and achiness permeated my body. I was still the sole parent and household manager. My neighbors watched the younger children when I went to regular physical therapy appointments and I could see that burdened their young homes but I was grateful for the help. I held onto the shopping carts at the grocery store with a death grip and the stair railing in our home with two hands to pull me up and down the stairs. I cried often. I don't know what the pain was, there was no relief anywhere.

I went for physical therapy and eventually over six month's time, I found relief. Maybe it was a transient virus, maybe it was the stress; there was no conclusion from the MRI – a good thing, really. The relief came as I found an outlet for me. I was hopeless for our situation, our marriage, the unmanaged emotions, the demand of our large family; I wanted to pursue my own dreams and I had to make a determination that there was hope still for us and a purpose for my struggling through the stress.

About that time, I got an invitation to go to my twentieth high school reunion and decided I would go, even if it meant I had to go by myself due to the current deployment. My neighbors, my extended family, kept the children for me so I could go for the long weekend.

It was a great time to reconnect with my friends from long ago, with my hopes and my dreams and who I was.

It was a time for refreshment and new perspective. Plus, it was simply fun to laugh and enjoy life again for that short weekend. When I returned I decided it was time to get back on track of the path of passion that was so important to me at an earlier time. It was time for me to find my healing and solutions to life's storms.

I had a long history of pageantry and acting. It was because of pageantry I had opportunities to volunteer and even go to college. I was the first of seven children to go to college because I competed in America's Junior Miss program and as second runner up at the state pageant, I received a full college scholarship. From seventh grade to married with children, I had been in about twenty five pageants and I had won or placed in every single one. I decided to find my strength in the beauty of a competition. As I did my research, I came across one that was a Christian pageant for married women who had a purpose and a passion (a platform).That was perfectly it. The Mrs. International pageant, on par with the well known Mrs. America pageant system would be a well-rounded, well-respected avenue for my pursuit of wellness and purpose.

It would give me a place to put my energy, focus on a disciplined, structured fitness program for restoring my health and provide an avenue for my *Spirit of America Days* program. With my husband still deployed, what better opportunity for me to use my time to do something productive and purposeful? I created an outline of how I would volunteer week by week, month by month in my community, what my fitness plan would look like and how I would prepare for my new goal.

I wanted to use this new goal of mine to be a role model for my children and to involve them in the giving. I thought about the different things I already did and considered how I could integrate our Fourth of July parades in our neighborhood and how I could activate the neighbors to volunteer further as we would adopted families for Christmas and put together baskets for people in our community. My children got valuable lessons on handing out food baskets to seniors through our church program and delivering turkeys with Catholic Charities. It was a great vehicle for widening my children's eyes and hearts to the opportunities of giving, volunteering, goal attainment and determination and how big goals, take a long time to achieve and timeline development and so on. They learned, too, about being productive in times of sadness, like when we were waiting for Dad's deployment to end, we could still be productive and useful.

I created the *Spirit of America Days* program to wake up America and our communities, but the best place to start was with me and my family and getting us to engage and volunteer in our communities.

I claimed the local title of Mrs. Newport News right away. I was sure of and determined for my goal, but I was a little uncomfortable about what my friends and neighbors might think about me competing for a pageant at such an age, so I busied myself with building the foundation of my plan of action and working on the *SAM* program and on Halloween, I announced it to my neighbors as I went trick or treating through the neighborhood with the children, wearing my new banner and small crown while collecting glasses for the Lions Club, for their Eyesight Trick or Treat program. It was a fun way to put it out there and to also maximize the event by collecting the glasses. I think everyone was both genuinely surprised and pleased.

Neighbors came together to support me in my endeavor and I worked toward my goal every day, determined to win the title in order that I might have an outlet for my program. Trick or treating was a fun, easy way to share the news with neighbors, but when it came to sharing my news with my husband, I knew it wouldn't be as easy. Letter writing and emails were our only avenues for communicating then. "I know you never really 'approved' of my pageants, but it is something I have to do for myself. I hope you will understand." Pageants were a mixed-bag for him. He never really liked me to do them, maybe the expense or the time commitment; I felt maybe it was a jealousy thing of my being out there for the world. Whatever the root, I know he had no affection for them, but he supported me and came to them when I competed, nonetheless.

He later shared that when he told his friends, he was initially disappointed at my decision, but when he told his friends thousands of miles away at his duty station in Afghanistan, their response changed his mind. "Good for you, your wife still has it together even after five kids." he told me they had said. "Good for you, she still wants to pursue something and do something." Eventually, he said, he mellowed and he accepted it, but I know he was never really pleased with my decision and he would confirm this later when I was on stage competing at Mrs. Virginia. I had just finished my evening gown competition walk, which I later won, and he said, "Darn. You did so well." I looked perplexed at his word choice and his delivery. He said," You looked so good, I know you are going to win, but I was hoping it was over."

He rarely understood my world. And it was further exacerbated at that time by the limit of our communications during deployment – limited to a few brief emails and short calls. Every day I was working toward my goal. I was creating bigger platforms and stronger messaging. I was volunteering and helping people in our community and was slowly gaining recognition for my community relations and the things that I was doing.

I was impacting the community and I was managing the family and the mounds of laundry and their school demands at the same time. All I would get was two or three line emails from him. His emails were the same almost always: "I miss you. I love you." That alone should have made me soar, but I needed more. I felt like he never really understood me or my world or how much I was managing or even hoping for. He wasn't a part of my world or what I was doing every day and I certainly wasn't a part of this war zone. There were no words to offer salve to our hurting hearts. There were no words of kudos or encouragement and the void became empty and big. I hoped for more in his emails every time. I wanted him to come home and be a part of our lives again. I wanted him in my world, in our marriage, along side of us. We were two married individuals, but living two different lives. We were separating at the seams.

CHAPTER THIRTEEN

DISARMED AND DISPOSED– THE THROW AWAY SOLDIER

There was a lot of stress in those emails from November to January and a lot of tears as I was trying to take care of the children and getting more tired every day without a break 24/7. They were more than simple, five is a big number alone, but also one child needed special care which was an hour away and the youngest had a very demanding medical condition that turned my world and the peace of our home upside down, as well. There was great physical and emotional demand at this stage and I was carrying that alone. I gained strength in the programs I was doing; the reprieve and the purpose was a great outlet. And the holidays were a great time to get everyone from my kids to my neighbors involved.

The holiday season, always especially hectic because it is also birthday season in our house, with four birthdays celebrated in a six week span, just as Thanksgiving and Christmas are kicking into gear, was a perfect time to get everyone involved and keep us distracted that our soldier Daddy would miss yet another Thanksgiving and Christmas at home.

Our family always celebrates Christmas in a big way and I used it as an opportunity to celebrate with neighbors and further my platform so I threw my annual Christmas party a little earlier in December and thirty or forty neighbors and kids were involved. Everybody came together for the purpose and the community.

We adopted a family. Kids and parents were in the kitchen and baked cookies. I had angels and ornaments and clothing I had shopped for earlier and the younger children helped to wrap them. It was a wonderful experience. My children learned about compassion and giving and charity and how a neighborhood can come together as we supported others in need. The true meaning of Christmas was vibrant in my home as everyone worked to contribute and bring a beautiful Christmas to a single mom of three little children. Everyone was blessed and not only was the Spirit of Christmas alive, but also the *Spirit of America* and it was healing for my tired spirit.

With the new year came news of our unit's return. The news, usually well received, was a message of mixed emotion for me. The tension between my husband and I was growing in our emails and we often ended up grumbling, even in our emails. I would say, "You don't understand what I am going through." And he would say, "But I love you – that's all that counts." He was right, but I was exhausted from all that was on my plate. And, yes, the program added more burdens, but it was also therapeutic, but household and medical demands and the burden of carrying it alone was the burden I needed relief from. And I wanted more from him–I wanted to connect on an emotional level. I wanted him to express his thoughts and his concern and understanding for me, not just his feelings for me and not just in one or two words or one or two sentences. I was looking for more to hold on to until all the madness would end.

I wanted him to have compassion and empathy for my situation. "I understand you are under a lot of pressure; I understand the children can be a handful. As soon as I get home I will be there to help. I will be there to carry the load with you. I see what you are doing and I know it's a lot. I appreciate what you are doing for our family and my career." Anything would have been

197

helpful. I just wanted him to say, "I see you. I know you are sacrificing a lot too. Thank you, I love you." But all I got was, "I miss you. I love you. Be home soon."

News of his return filled me with sadness and dread, not relief. Though we had not voiced it on the phone the very few times we talked and we had seen it on the emails, it was just an unacknowledged elephant in the room (or on the computer). I was sad, frustrated, burdened and was often further disappointed when I would learn that other people could make phone calls easily and often and he very rarely made phone calls to me. Did he not think of us? Did he not remember that we were battling through our own days without him for him?

News of the reunion brought on a sadness because it was time to face the pain and fill the void this deployment and all the deployments before had created. There was no joy in the retirement that I hoped would come because our future had lost its luster. The emails had elevated as I finally put it some of my feelings in an email so he would know what needed to be addressed. It was nearing time for the reunion and it had to be said. His response wasn't to address my feelings or acknowledge my position, but to say, "Come or don't come, it doesn't matter to me, but I'll be arriving on January 18th. I don't even want you to come."

How ludicrous. Of course I was coming! Of course we missed him. In spite of the frustration or bickering, we–I–still loved him. My gosh, he was a soldier coming home from war, of course, we would make the drive to Fort Bragg and be there for his homecoming. Of course we would work this out, somehow. His attitude, his dismissal, just irritated me further, but of course, we were going.

He greeted the kids somberly and nearly overlooked me. He hugged me half-heartedly. He said, "I really didn't think you were coming. I didn't expect you to be here." And after a brief reunion, he went about finishing up his business and his goodbyes and we headed to Virginia to home. You wouldn't have guessed we had just been separated by a deployment and the homecoming was rather anti-climatic.

My sister wanted to give us the gift of time when he returned, so she flew in from Texas to watch the kids, so he and I could enjoy some quiet time at the Homestead in Virginia. The transition is always difficult when the soldier arrives. And while everyone is clamoring to be seen and heard and to connect, it was especially important for us to retreat to connect after this deployment. And, he arrived home just as it was our 15th anniversary and a good purpose for a get-away.

It was tense and awkward and tenuous; there was a huge barrier between us and we would have to overcome that in short order if we were going to reintegrate success-fully. Certainly, just time together would help ease our wounds and fears and, if nothing else, we would have an opportunity start speaking and communicating. We had a great time; the Homestead is a fabulous property and a great resort, but I recognized then that there was unusual tension that wouldn't be worked out in a weekend.

He would often wave me away when I would try to approach him and show my affection. This was not the husband that had left. This was not the husband that I knew; the husband always looking for my attention. We had a peaceful and serene weekend, but the disconnect was obvious.

The union at home was not much better; irrational behaviors and comments were common. For example, on the way home from our weekend, I shared that I had purchased the boys golf clubs for Christmas. He was quite agitated with me and admonished me saying, "Why would you do that? You're setting them up for a life their never going to have." He was not at all happy with that purchase.

But at home it increased to more explosive levels, discontentedness quickly became flashpoint anger and there was an incident of extreme irrational thinking involving grade reports and the kids and I ran to get the reports and was trying to make sense of the injustice and he was not receiving the information and the anger and rage elevated to an intense, scary level before the door bell rang from a neighbor and we were able to walk away. He quickly turned from the intensity to the calm, cool, collected door man and we simply retreated after that. There was nothing easy about reintegration for a military family.

There was also an expectation of being gone and showing up as if nothing had change, no roles had changed, an expectation that feelings and emotions could be flipped on and off like a light switch and that the entire period of separation could be ignored or not acknowledged. It was an irrational way of thinking and it caused conflict every time upon return.

Within a few short weeks, the Army had finally agreed to release him and we were planning his retirement. There would be a ceremony and a retirement celebration was in order. For whatever reason, his family had decided not to attend his retirement ceremony, so I decided to take the opportunity prior to his actual ceremony to create a very special family getaway, including his folks, to celebrate all that had been his and our military career.

I found a place in Maggie Valley in the mountains and invited his family to join our family after the ball. There was to be a military ball and because of his impending retirement, he was going to be the master of ceremonies. He was spotlighted to mix the symbolic officer's punch; it was quite exciting. I picked out an evening gown and he was going to wear his dress blues. It was a ball, so we started calling it the prom and did all the things prom kids do. We were actually looking forward to it and welcomed the reprieve from the anger and the ticking time bomb at home.

I had my hair and nails done and he was excited to pick out a satin, strapless gown with me. Not one that I would have picked for myself, but something that he envisioned me in and I was happy to wear it for him. His parents came up from Florida to join us and they were happy to be going to the mountains following the ball. It was actually a lovely time for us and had promise of the transition slipping behind us, but while we were at the event, he didn't spend a great deal of time with me at our table. I recall one great dance and he seemed very happy to be at the event, but we basically moved through the festivities on our own.

He was engaged with his military comrades as they shared stories of their overseas events and I was there to look like the prom queen. Somehow, that night and the weekend to come was almost our goodbye. We had a lovely time, the kids enjoyed the mountain house. The mother in law cooked and showed the granddaughter how to knit and the kids and I played games. He and I took a walk in the woods and he insisted on taking pictures of me. His father captured a beautiful one which his mother later framed and presented to us of a rainbow over the mountains, but there would be no rainbow. I insisted we spend time talking about my thoughts and dreams and hopes of things that were important to me and he was very angry at listening, almost as if he were angry because of who I was and what I wanted from life and life after retirement. He stewed after that and when we returned home and said goodbye to his family, the anger bubbled up again. Soon it was time for his actual retirement and his ceremony at his last duty post of Fort Bragg. Again, he said, "Come or don't come, I don't really care."

But of course I was coming; *we* earned this – him, me, each one of the children. This retirement ceremony was for me and each of the children as much as it was for him. My mother flew in from Florida, having been so much a part of his career and our family during our long journey. My mother, the children and I drove to Fort Bragg together, yet not one of his family members would come. Not one of his family members came to such an important event – he had made the effort on more than one occasion for them, for family events, and yet not one came; my mother and I thought this very odd. One sister- in- law who happened to live at Fort Bragg with Vincent's brother who was also stationed there, but deployed at that time joined us and for lunch following.

We were grateful she had arrived; it was more than just the awkwardness of us. The ceremony was simple and brief; there was very little fanfare. He was ash grey and didn't look like he was accepting it very well, more like he was receiving a funeral flag instead of a medal of his service. I knew then that it was a mistake that I had asked him to retire, but I knew I could not endure one more day of what had rocked our world and upset our plans for a beautiful future together. In that moment, we had to go through the motions and the ceremony. Even there, I was full of perplexity. After twenty three years of service, this is what it was like to receive honor? It was almost without fanfare, another life event to chalk up to all the experience and sacrifice–an event done.

After fifteen years of being married to him in the military, this is what it was like to be thanked? I was wounded again. It was a simple thank you, a simple recognition – but a moment in time. We stood up in formation with a few other couples and received our rewards in succession. It was a bit of acknowledgment from the military, a tilt of the hat. For the family there was no extra honor or congratulations; the children had given and sacrificed and endured much, too, and yet, no recognition–maybe there was a "and their families" mention that I have since forgotten, but no fanfare. And again, maybe because we had not adopted Fort Bragg as our duty station, there was no military community of Army wives to cheer us on or share in our excitement and accomplishment as we had known in our previous duty stations. The recognition was Army-issued and simple that day. I was grateful my mother was there.

Following the very brief ceremony, we went to dinner at a Japanese steakhouse. I was grateful that the sister-in-law was there to break the tension and make conversation with the children. The children seemed amiable and happy to be there, but it was like a funeral for the adults at the table. It was not really like a celebration where you retire and everyone is patting you on the back and congratulating you, no, it was something we were enduring until the moment of explosion, which we each sensed was on the horizon, the moment you can no longer ignore that elephant.

Before we had played taps for the day, it escalated to something much worse and the anger was released into the atmosphere. After dinner we returned to the hotel where we had two adjoining rooms; one for the children and my mother and one for my husband and me. The anger just bubbled over and there was no putting a lid on it; he was overwhelmed and it came spewing out. Everything he had known that was familiar to him was now gone. He would no longer be connected to the military. For him, it was a day of dishonor. Every bit of pain, every root of bitterness, every bit of frustration and anger bubbled up between us and erupted in our hotel room, with the adjoining door open and every family member sitting around in audience.

The fact that I was involved in the Mrs. Virginia pageant was aggravating him; the fact that I was doing something good and not mourning with him, was aggravating him. He escalated to the point of hot rage and he was bellowing at the top of his lungs even in the hotel room.

We were unwinding from the day, changing our celebration clothes and I told him I was going to maximize the time and mileage of this trip to stop on the way back to see a coach for my pageant preparation. We had two family cars with us, so I suggested I would drive home with my mother so we could make this brief detour of a half day to meet a pageant coach and he would take the children with him and drive home ahead.

He was very upset he had to be with the children – that I was 'dumping them on him so I could go off and party' and I also think he was grasping for a way to control that I was in this pageant to dissuade me from pursuing something other than him. He was personally offended that I was combining the trips, saying that it minimized the importance of his retirement ceremony, that I only came as an obligation, but I was really there for the purpose of this side trip. I think he was deeply wounded that there was something good happening for me and yet he was mourning something that was very important to him. He was grasping at straws and he was throwing darts at me.

"We will be getting a divorce after this! This will end our marriage," he screamed at the top of his lungs, red in the face, with the kids sitting around the room and tears running down my face.

But, how could I begin to assume what it meant for him? All I know is that retirement day which should have been our greatest joy, after dedicating 16 years of our lives and sacrificing so much – the greater joy of our family, was nothing more than a funeral. A funeral for our marriage, a funeral for our family and a funeral for the military he loved so much. On that day we parted ways, even though it would be years before we would find the courage to walk away. He took the children and headed home and my mother and I headed toward our destination sharing the pain for what had just trans-pired and the wounds inflicted in this most recent and serious conflict.

CHAPTER FOURTEEN

WAR RAGES ON AND I WILL NOT SURRENDER

F ollowing retirement, we still had to function in at our home and determine how our retirement transition would unfold. He had unused leave and was off-duty, but still receiving benefits for four months. He was able to find a contract job supporting a government contract and a military mission at nearby Fort Monroe, Virginia.

I continued to pursuing my goal of the crown. I had been working diligently on my goal for seven months at this point and I was committed to organizations for volunteering. I was in the capacity of Mrs. Newport News and I was still preparing for Mrs. Virginia. At this point,

I was quite connected in the community and everyone knew of my big goal.

When we returned from the retirement ceremony to our home in Virginia, I felt like such a hypocrite competing for such a title when our world was falling apart, but I had not yet decided to do on any level.

Whenever my husband would enter a room, he was chastising the children or picking a battle with one of us. I was constantly trying to diffuse the emotion and all the while trying to make progress toward my goal and the SAM program I believed in. I had already earned my first congressional endorsement from a U.S. Representative and I was not eager to walk away in haste.

The tension was constant and sporadically would erupt at home, everyone simply trying to go through their daily motions. Each child seemed to have their own struggle whether academic, emotional, physical or simply growing pains – there was a lot going on and a lot to juggle and address at any one time.

In between I persisted in my goals–dressing up and going to community events, volunteering for various organizations, home cooking meals and taking care of the children and the house–but there would be an ongoing battle and unrest in every room of the house. And when it was directed toward my cubs, well, you have seen a momma bear protecting her cubs; I played interference many, many times trying to reason our way through the situation.

The pressure finally got to me and at the seven month point I wrote a letter to the state director of my pageant system. I felt like such a hypocrite. I couldn't tell them the whole truth, but I had to tell them something. I wrote them a letter to resign. I told them I would no longer pursue the crown. It didn't make sense in my head, competing for a crown while my house was crumbling; competing to be a role model for married women when my house was in turmoil. I told them it was a critical point for my family after his return and impending retirement and I couldn't continue.

I received the most awesome letter in return–a letter of encouragement and support. *We will help you with whatever it takes, but you have what it takes. We believe in you, we believe in your message. We want this for you and your family–we implore you to stay and continue with the competition.*

And so I did. Nothing improved at home, but somehow I felt like I was meant to do this. I received encouragement along the way and I was gaining momentum wherever I went in the community and my reach was going further now. I reached out for a mentor after crossing paths with the Director of the National Patient Advocate Foundation and she was quick to take me under her wing. She was a woman wiser than me who had much wisdom to give. She was a figure in the community making a difference in people's lives. She was quite gracious.

I wanted to model my program after someone who had success with a similar program model and she took me under her wing. I used this to gain courage for the bigger competition ahead. The Mrs. Tennessee pageant was held simultaneously, everyone competing for their own state. What a fantastic gathering of beautiful women. We spent a week rehearsing, preparing, gathering and competing. Our families were invited to be a part of it. My husband would even wear his dress blues and be welcomed on stage with me both during competition and for my crowning moment.

The children were there, all polished and pressed, and my mother came to help. I was proud to have my family there and my husband dressed up so sharp in his uniform, but I was on edge during those moments, not sure of what might be said–things not congruent or to be aired publicly or that tempers might flair. So much time spent in the military can blur the boundaries or things can come off rough or unedited.

Finally, the day of competition and crowning had arrived. I could soon be wearing the crown and have a voice for my platform. I wanted this to get the message of

Spirit America Days out. I wanted to give back. I wanted this for my children. I wanted this for myself.

I really wanted all of the skills, talents and experiences that I had acquired to somehow come together and fit together and make sense somewhere, somehow to someone and be important and make a difference in my community, for others, in my world. Somehow in the recognition, that I would get back some of what was lost–my career along the way, the stress, the sacrifice; that there would be just a hint of recognition and validation and a moment for just me.

I took my final walk in my evening gown that night and felt confident. I went backstage feeling especially excited and my husband stood there in his military uniform. He took me and wrapped me around his arms and said, "Darn! You did so good. I wanted this to be the end, but you did too good. I know you are going to win."

It was sweet, but a funny way of congratulating me. It was a bittersweet way of telling me that I was beautiful to him, but it was something he didn't want for our lives. I went on stage and he waited in the wings with the other spouses. When they announced my name, I was shaking. I put down my plaques of Evening Gown Competition Winner and Overall State Fitness Winner just minutes before the final announcement because in my heart of hearts I just knew I was going to win.

Not because I had done anything better than any of the other ladies on stage, but because I knew this was my moment–finally. This was my redeeming moment and God leaned down from heaven and said, "Yes Jackie, I see you. I see how hard you have worked and I want to honor you. Here's your moment – take your walk, daughter; dry your tears."

But the tears came anyway. I was shaking and crying tears of joy and relief and disbelief as my husband came to put that beautiful state crown on me. I couldn't stop shaking and thanking God for this moment, for this dream to come true for me. It was to be a short-lived fairy tale as we gathered our things the next day. I was still floating on air from the victory, but the battlefield was still ahead of me. My mother and I rode home with the children in the van and my husband rode separately because we had two cars to take home.

That ride home was tumultuous and stressful and we hadn't even yet arrived home. He was constantly texting me, trying to control our pace. The rage was constant. "Hurry up! Speed up! Stay with us!" He would say. I was uncomfortable pushing the limits of the set speed limit. He would call me and berate me on the phone; he wasn't pleased with my victory, the stress of all the baggage and the kids and he wanted to get home.

I can't remember the exact exchange, but it was constant and we were battling.

We stopped for gas along the way. As I pulled up to the pump for gas, my husband pulled further away, off to the side, away from the pumps. He came out of his car, got my son out of the car and was yelling at him in this public parking lot. I could see my son shuddering from his distress.

I didn't even know what it was about, but I could see the rage of a warrior–did he not realize this was a child he loved? He was towering over my son with his height and had his arm twisted behind his back and I remember putting the fuel pump down and demanding for him to let go and get in the car.

It all transpired very quickly and I couldn't make sense of any of it. We were soon on our way back home. The rage continued as my husband called us on the cell phone repeatedly throughout our drive. I was shaking and I knew, although I had just won a crown and I was pursuing my dreams to reach to the Mrs. International level, which was only seven weeks away and the Miss America dreams of my childhood – that was no longer important.

As news of my victory was hitting the newspaper, as neighbors were coming over with flowers to congratulate me, as my two dozen lavender roses which symbolized my victory on my kitchen table blossomed, I knew that we had reached a point of no return. I was very clear to my husband that night that we would not take one more step forward until he agreed to join us for counseling. And the very next day we were in the counselor's office, where the local paper was sitting on the coffee table with my crowning picture of victory face up. But that office visit would begin the change of something good; something good in my husband where he finally understood a bit about parenting and where we were able to find our first light of relief. Reaching out for the help he needed was the right thing to do. I would like to thank that counselor for the difference he made.

Now I am not saying by any stretch that it was a miracle healing. It's just the first time I can recall my husband hearing anything that seemed to make a difference in our situation. The counselor saw my husband, he saw me, he saw us separately and together and eventually he would see each of the children – so he got the full view of life at home. Whatever wise words that counselor offered to my husband was something that would take root and give my husband a shift in his view of how he parented the boys. It would be a few more years and a lot more turmoil before he would make the shift with the girls. He often reverted to trying to control us the way the military controlled him as a soldier, but it wasn't an effective leadership style and was disintegrating our family.

He learned that day that he could no longer bully the boys or challenge them face to face, chest to chest the way a drill sergeant would train up a military soldier. He could no longer command us the way the military commanded the soldiers. We were not little soldiers, we were not the military, and we were not the enemy. Our home was not a battlefield. And thank the Lord this beautiful counselor in his campy, comfortable, easy way would reach my husband and bring the slightest amount of hope.

It was then that my husband began to bond with the boys. There was a small shift for a time. It would not defuse the anger over night, we would still be prisoners in our own home, but a shift had occurred and the beginning of a relationship had been initiated. With that attended to, I continued on my way to pursue the title of Mrs. International because, one thing you learn in the military is – life goes on, even when battles rage around you, life goes on and time passes by.

Seven weeks later I competed for Mrs. International and my entire family came up from Florida to cheer me on. The kids came sporting little tuxedoes and evening gowns. They were so precious, but I was very scheduled and didn't have much interaction. My husband wore his dress blues and joined me on stage for the couples dance. We were able to make small talk.

Out of 51 states and countries represented, I would place in the Top Ten. Even though I wouldn't take home the crown, I would have given a voice to *Spirit of America Days* and found a path to give it momentum in the near future. But, bigger still, I would have been a role model for my daughters and my children and demonstrate to them that in the midst of calamity, pursue your dreams, never, never, never give up. In the midst of abnormality, you can find your normal. And in the midst of dysfunction, find a way to function. Find a way to love one another, a way to hang on, to persevere and also, to pursue what you believe in. I'm glad I did that. I'm glad I spoke up to get the counseling that was so needed. I'm glad I spoke up when I felt as if I were a hypocrite, but I'm glad I persisted in the face of so much turmoil. It would have been equally sad for that to be taken from me, too. In the end, I found an avenue for both *Spirit of America Days* and my spirit to thrive.

CHAPTER FIFTEEN

HALLELUJAH! FSBO FREES
PRISONERS IN FIVE DAYS

My husband had finally gotten contract work after being unemployed. His greatest fear after military retirement was that he would have no income. We were grateful for the contract. It wasn't exactly a position he wanted, but it was at Fort Monroe in a military environment. Only thirty minutes from our home–not a bad commute.

It still was not what he wanted, we knew it was temporary. The contract was to be for six months, but after four months the military pulled the contract and he was once again without work – twice in a six month period and the first time in his adult life he had ever experienced unemployment; the military is a secure job. He

218

was devastated. We were at a point of loss and I should have shared in his devastation, but I was thrilled. When most people would cry and moan, I said, "Hallelujah!" Finally, we have our opportunity to pursue our dream of moving to Florida and being near our families; we have freedom over our own lives now.

We put our house up for sale by owner after a brief discussion. My bargain was that if he would agree to allow me to market and sell the house, I could use the money I saved on paying a realtor to buy Disneyworld season passes for our family. To live in Florida and take my children to Disneyworld everyday–to finally live a happy, joyful life of our choosing–this was my dream. I saw this as a God send, not a disappointment to be feared or mourned.

He agreed, so I put up a sign, made flyers, cleaned up the house and staged it just right, and I started showing our house. Only God can move mountains like this: in five days, we sold our house by owner, and it was not a seller's market. It was a miracle.

He lived up to his promise and allowed me to take some of that equity profit and buy season passes. It was an expensive venture, but it would be our life saver for the summer ahead. We went to Florida, where my dream was to live, but it was to be the most unusual year in Florida's history in a long time. In 2004, we moved on

May 13th. It was a challenging move but the military helped us and we were able to do it.

It was sad to say goodbye to a community we loved. We had a picnic; our children cried, I cried. We were all very sad to let go of those bonds. They had become the family that helped us survive, but the door was shut on employment opportunities and I was turning it into an opportunity to pursue my dream–the dream I thought would be perfect for my family.

When we arrived in Florida, the hurricane started – an unprecedented five hurricanes in one year. We headed to my brother's house in Orlando, FL and bounced around several other family homes chasing or outrunning hurricanes as we tried to find a place to settle. My brother had a large beautiful house with a pool in the shape of Mickey Mouse and it was a good place to start our journey.

As soon as we arrived, he took us to Brios restaurant for a celebration dinner and welcomed the entire family to Florida. I woke up with the sun shining; grateful for having arrived. I could not wait to embrace what lay ahead. Soon, we had news of hurricanes on the horizon and one after another they came. We went to South Florida and there was a hurricane that followed us there, too.

My older brother, Glenn, was boarding up his house. When the hurricane finally passed, we went to the nearby town where we thought he would have a job opportunity. They had talked about this job offer for my husband for two years, but when we arrived they said "Sorry, we have decided the person that fills the position must know Portuguese." Portuguese? What a unique language. He certainly didn't know Portuguese, so that dream was dashed.

We traveled to see his brother in Port St. Richey, and sure enough, another hurricane had just blown through and there was debris everywhere. We returned to Orlando, and yet another hurricane pounded the region. And in similar fashion, the family was being torn apart by emotional hurricanes at home. First, he had left the military and he was sad every day that he had, but now he had lost his job and he went into a deep depression, never having been unemployed before .

He was not able to engage and look for a job. I tried to motivate him every day. But instead, he would retreat to the room with the remote and the television. He would retreat from the children and instead of engaging, he would brood or take care of himself or whatever I asked him to do. He had drawn an emotional barrier between his family and him.

We had to go to his niece's graduation in Port St. Richey and we packed the car and headed that direction yet again. By that time, there was so much anger and rage as we talked about what our life would be like.

Where would we go? Where would we put down roots? I didn't want to pursue a job offer for myself because it was harder to get a job as a helicopter pilot and so with that thinking, I thought a job offer for him should lead our direction to move.

I wanted him to take the lead. As we headed to his nieces graduation, war raged in the car. The children were crying, I was crying; I begged him to stop. I begged for us to end this constant arguing and fighting. There was no peace the entire trip and when we arrived, that would be the trip that would mark the line in the sand– our final separation. The crack would grow bigger in our marriage in the foundation we had set. The enemy lines would be drawn around the kitchen table and he would be the one to make the mark; I simply called his bluff.

As we sat around the kitchen table at my sister-in-law's house, she at the head, my husband at the other head and me next to my husband's side, there was one or two children at the table with us and the others were playing throughout the house. I remember looking at my sister-in-law and saying, "Kris, where is your wedding ring?" And she said, "Oh, it bothers me, I take it off from time to time. I put it on my bed side, I have to take it off every night."

I started rubbing my fingers and I said, "Funny. My hands are swollen, too, but I never take mine off." As I tried to pull on it, it tugged at my knuckle and I realized my hands were really swollen; probably all of the travel and not drinking enough water. So I tugged and I tugged and I finally I was able to get it over my swollen knuckle and I took off the ring, laid it on the table and started rubbing my hands. I felt such relief as I wiggled my fingers back to full circulation.

I said, "Oh, I would never take off my ring. Vince would never tolerate it." And sure enough, he reached down and he snatched up my ring off the table from where I had just laid it. He said, "You will never take this ring off again." And I looked at him and I said, "You can't tell me that. Give me my ring back." But he refused. A small, quiet argument ensued as we all sat around the table, but he stood firm and had decided not to give me my ring back.

In that moment, I knew that I would never wear my ring again. I didn't want it back. I didn't want to be married to somebody who wanted to control me, where we live in constant enemy territory and a battle zone where there was no respect and so little love. I didn't want to be married to somebody like that. I was to be free in my marriage; I was free to love him, he couldn't tell me to love him–he didn't own me. And in that moment, it was all fully punctuated for me and that was the line in the sand for me.

We returned to Orlando without my ring on my finger. No one noticed, but he and I knew. It became a big story for us. I returned to Orlando with five children and a husband with no job, but truly, no spouse. In fact, I told him not to even bother to come inside the house and he drove to Jacksonville to stay at his mother's house.

We were in Orlando, but the children missed him. He called every day and wanted to come back. I was weak still and I couldn't firmly say no, even if I felt it in my heart. I really just wanted him to find a job, I wanted him to take action for our family and I wanted him to care; I wanted him to wake up to the family that wanted him to love us. I wanted him to engage, to change, to let go of all of the anger that he had bottled up–the result of years and years of battle.

The kids and I went to my brother's house, but he was ready to claim his own space again, with less commotion and his own routine. With great timing, his next door neighbors were going to be out of state for a month and extended us an invitation to live in their house – if we wouldn't mind. We could take care of their house so it wouldn't be vacant for so long and have a home to ourselves. That was such a gift. I will be forever grateful for the month we had in that home.

My husband returned to join us when we moved in to the house next door. But still there was no cohesion.

I stayed in the room with my youngest daughter who didn't like to be away from me and the children kind of flowed in and out of the rooms between my husband and me. There was definitely a boundary, a wall, a barrier between us and it was fragmenting the family.

We were strangers living in a stranger's house and he was despondent and disengaged. He barely looked for a job, occasionally on the computer, but never in the newspaper, never knocking on doors or feeling out the environment. Mostly he just thought a job would come looking for him. I think he was helpless not knowing how to engage after the military had told him what to do for so many years.

Perhaps this was PTSD and I didn't even know what it looked like. But for me, it was just a depressed, despondent man who wouldn't take control for his family. I had tried to distract my children. I tried to love them through it and live through, denying the reality. We went to Disney World every day. He went once or twice, but he wasn't really happy to be there.

He hated theme parks. The excitement was overwhelming, the distraction and the constant sensory overload irritated him. We went on our own and we enjoyed the fun of it. My younger son wasn't always thrilled about having to take pictures and walk along in the heat with little money to offer us freedom for purchasing, but overall, my children were happy to be at Disney World and I was happy to be spending time with them.

We loved being at the Magic Kingdom and taking the safari at Animal Kingdom. In fact, we stayed at the Animal Kingdom Lodge the first weekend we arrived, using our season . My husband did enjoy that part of the trip, but he would have no part of the season passes at the park the rest of the summer.

After the move next door, we were now three months without a home; nearly homeless with five kids in the heat of the summer. The air conditioning had gone out in the van and my husband was resistant to spending the money to get it fixed. I realized our relationship was like that, he wasn't willing to make the investment to repair the tension there either. I could never help him fight his own battle or help him make sense of where we were. He would have to go out and find himself, to be a better father and husband and to keep our family together.

Soon after, I brought my children in the backyard by the pool and I sat them around the table and I told them, "This was it." I told them, "We can't seem to resolve all the issues and we are going to go in separate directions and make the move on our own."

He had an opportunity to go to Louisiana and one to go to Charleston, but he couldn't make a choice. He was afraid I wouldn't follow like when I hadn't followed him to Fort Bragg. But that was different; that was the military and another post assignment. This would be a life for us together post-retirement, of course I would follow. Neither location was where I wanted to go, but I would follow. We didn't have many options – I just wanted one option, any option. But at the time of decision, I couldn't say for sure how fully committed I was because I couldn't say for certain that he would let go of the anger and that there would be any change, any hope for our family or our future.

I told the children that night that it was time, "Daddy would be moving out and we would not be moving on together." There were tears. But what caused me to have a change of heart was my then, eleven year old daughter, a child of great wisdom.

She looked at my then, five year old daughter and said, "Mommy, you can't leave. She doesn't even know him." And she was right. He had never taken time to engage with the youngest daughter. She was constantly vomiting and in full reflux for a full year as a baby. Then she displayed her anger and her frustration for another year, causing turmoil and upset in every room of the house. She was a child who needed the full attention of her mommy.

By the third year, she started becoming healthy and whole. He was gone, transitioned to Fort Bragg and then deployed to Afghanistan. After his return, she was clinging to her mother who had nursed her through poor health for the first two years of her little life. She clung to me making it harder for him to get close. I was her primary care giver and the only one she really warmed up to. He didn't engage with her; he did not know her. My Kaitlin was right. How could I leave when these children were so little and didn't really have a strong relationship with their father?

Chapter Sixteen

Living in a War Zone

He did go to investigate the job in Louisiana but went back to Jacksonville. The parting words he said to me as we were in the backyard of my brother's house, just he and I saying our goodbyes through the tears, he said, "I want you to have your wedding ring back before I leave."

I said, "I don't want it back. You took it from me and held it hostage and that wasn't right and now, I don't ever want that ring back."

He pressed on, "I want you to have it," and he pressed it into the palm of my hand and clasped my fingers over it. I refused to put it on after that, but I did take it. It held so much meaning. It was my greatest joy at one time, but now too many painful memories and it

229

signified what was broken and forever lost. I put it into a special box and I would never wear it again. He left me standing in the doorway at my brother's house and he even had his friends call me to try and figure out whether I would follow him on that job or not. In the end, he didn't take the position and instead went to stay at his mother's house.

We had friends from Germany that lived in Peachtree City, Georgia and they invited us to come investigate and stay with them, "This is Candy Land! This place is 'the bubble'. It's great for kids. You will love it here." At this point I didn't know which choices to make, what was the right decision; we had no house, I was a single mother yet again, but this time it looked like it would be permanent role for me.

I agreed to go to Peachtree City because while I wanted to be with my mother, my siblings and my cousins, I didn't want my children to fear the crime in South Florida. The schools went from A's to D's in their ratings; it wasn't a healthy environment for grade school children, in my opinion. There was no place we really fit. I knew it wasn't a place I wanted to raise my children and so with sadness, I said goodbye and we headed to Georgia to temporarily live with my friend until I could make some decisions. She invited us into her home. She had two daughters and her husband who were all so warm and welcoming. We went there and I prayed in the neighborhood parks looking for answers, "Was this the right place for us? Was I meant to leave my dream of Florida and live in Georgia?" Georgia was a state I was never fond of; a place I had never connected with – our car broke down in Georgia when I was on a family trip as a little girl and I had never let go of that memory.

It seemed like a great place to raise a family. The schools were great, the community looked warm and welcoming and we had this beautiful family that said we could live with them while we transitioned. I prayed and prayed about it and I finally concluded that it must be the right decision. During my decision-making my friend thought she would play the matchmaker and unbeknownst to me, invited my husband for dinner one night. He just showed up.

It was unnerving, but I tried to make peace for the children. I tried to pretend that I didn't care he was there, but I did. I didn't want him there, I was angry. I wanted to move on, I wanted to separate and divorce and be done; I wanted it and all of our problems and pain to go away. I wanted to be done with the anger, with the verbal abuse, the confusion and indecision. But there he was. I know my girlfriend meant well, but I wasn't happy by the surprise attack.

Sure enough, the kids were excited their daddy was back, they thought It meant our family was repaired. So, I agreed to take one for the team one more time to give him an opportunity to parent his children, an opportunity for them to get to know him. Sure enough, there would be one more time, but there still would be no peace. I put my hope in this transition, in the bubble, in the house that was to come, but our marriage had so very little hope.

I said if we could find a house in the same neighborhood, I would make it work. There were three or four houses for sale and we kept hoping for more. We looked every day. We looked in the pouring rain even. Then there was a rainbow of hope when within a few days of him being at Peachtree City, he was offered a job at the nearby airfield with Air Rescue.

I knew then that it had to be a sign; we were meant to be here and I would do everything to make it work. If this is what it took for our family to be together, I was determined to do it. I vowed never to get a divorce, so this seemed like an opportunity to try again–what I was meant to do. We went to the first house and made them an offer, but they were not going to budge to our lower than the asking price offer.

We went to the second house and looked at it multiple times. The house had many walls dividing the rooms and flow of the house and I didn't like it. It had a basement and my children thought it would be wonderful to live in a house where they could hide out in the basement. The boys wanted to live in the basement. After multiple times of looking at it, knowing that it didn't feel quite settled in my spirit, but with so few options, I agreed.

We made an offer: fifteen thousand dollars below asking price and to our surprise, they accepted it. After seven weeks of living in my friend's house and of their graciousness and hospitality, we moved to a house down the street, into our own home. But instead of the welcome wagon, we were welcomed by a terrible tragedy on moving day.

It would become the darkest days of our life; seven months of living in yet another war zone, a battlefield indeed, but of another kind. The day we moved in was my fortieth birthday. I had planned for several years to be celebrating in New York City with my sisters and my mother. We were going to Broadway, we were going to toast champagne, but instead it was the day the Army had assigned as our military move.

On that day, I would be receiving twenty five thousand pounds of household goods off two and a half eighteen wheelers, dripping wet. You see, there was a leak in the moving van and it rained just a day or two before while the truck was sitting in front of our new home.

It took three days to offload all of the goods and after it rained, the next day was hot, humid and steamy in Southern Georgia. The goods, tightly packed together, created moisture and a steam that created mold and mildew in these boxes that held our life's possessions.

As they offloaded all of the boxes into our house, as the days advanced, the boxes created and emitted a mold and mildew that was toxic. I purchased a mold tester at Home Depot, and the mold that grew was fuzzy green and white and black and toxic. My children were transitioning under all of this stress from the move, from the loss of friends and stability; they were sick and coughing and sneezing and we couldn't determine what it was. As soon as I confirmed the mold, we no longer slept on the beds or sat on the couches–we slept on the floors for four months following those tests.

After having missed a month of school, my kids began school in each of their respective four different schools: the elementary, the middle school, the high school and the preschool. We went to sleep crying every night as I made pallets on the floor, not understanding why there was no solution. My husband sat in a recliner, night after night, watching TV. He never tried to unload a single box. He never tried to offer a solution. He simply disconnected from the turmoil.

He went into a deep depression. I had to quickly become the military voice for our family. Even though the military doesn't issue a spouse, they had to learn to deal with this spouse. I went to the JAG (legal) office and filled out forms that they gave me after I explained our situation. I begged them for help. After a month of time and persistence, they finally came to the house and agreed, the boxes were moldy with mildew and damaged.

They sent moving professionals to unload the boxes but all they would authorize was the cutting of the tape and an emptying of the boxes–upside down in their place. In four thousand square feet of home, from floor to floor, it looked like an active war zone. From papers and China, to household goods collected over twenty three years, a retirement move had become our demise.

This was the end of the materialism in our house and when God showed up to rid us of any attachment to things. So many of our goods were destroyed, damaged or not worth keeping. I started sorting them and taking them to the garage but the garage was soon packed and overflowing. Slowly, I sifted through the disaster and organized, refurbished or disposed of our belongings. It had a terrible impact on my children. And I was overwhelmed and sad every day from the task that lay ahead.

The children were sad, they couldn't engage with friends, the community was not warm and welcoming to make new friends. It was eight months before they would start making truly good friends, which they would then have as lifelong friends. This community would become our family once again, but it would take eight full months of isolation and loneliness.

In seven months of time, I catalogued everything in our house. I searched the internet for price comparisons. I filled out forms for insurance. I found people who would appraise our goods. I took pictures and I restored the house to a living state.

Concurrently, I engaged the children in their schools and helped them with their academic struggles. I helped them make new friends, I made sure we got to church on time on Sundays, I made home cooked meals and tried to conduct a normal flow of life. Yet, the stress mounted as my husband never engaged and the kids noted his absence and I sunk deeper into regret and hopelessness myself.

After two months of sleeping in a rocking chair, I felt so sad for him I went out while he was at work and purchased a room full of furniture and furnished the basement. Two beds, a beautiful red couch and a brand new place for him to watch TV. I cleaned up the basement, painted it and created a beautiful billiards and poker theme in it.

When he came home, instead of being grateful for having a bed to sleep on, he said he would never sleep on those beds because he didn't want to make the beds, but mostly because he didn't want to know that I had kicked him out of his house and created a space for him to permanently live in. That wasn't my intent at all.

He took it all wrong. I just wanted him to be comfortable; I couldn't stand to see him sad and sleeping in that chair every day. I wanted to give him hope so that he would want to reengage again. I wanted him to have a bed in the same way I had a bed to sleep on. I wanted the children to see that he had a decent living space. I really wanted him to engage in our house–I wanted him to walk up the stairs and take leadership of the family as I expected him to.

I wanted him to provide the covering and the spiritual leadership for our home. But he couldn't do it. He couldn't find the strength within himself. He was a worn out soldier, having seen too much on the battlefield, having been engaged in a war zone for too long. He had given up the fight.

He had been told what to do by the military for years upon years. He was lost and didn't know how to re-engage. Likely a victim of PTSD, but all I saw was the anger, rage and disconnectedness that indicated so many more things, certainly indicated a pulling away from the family.

There was so much sadness in our home. I constantly took our children aside and said, "Your daddy is sick and he is making us sick, too. We have to learn how to function in this dysfunction. It's not normal what we go through in our home. When you grow up, you do not have to be this way. You make a choice to be a strong father. You make a choice to show up differently.

"You make a choice to go to church and be a good spiritual leader. You make a choice to love your wife and your children. Right now, Daddy is sick and we will just have to be patient with him, but we have to take care of ourselves in this time. Just stay out of the way as much as possible. "

All the while, I would look for moments of escape. I would pack our suitcases and our bags and put them in the trunk of our car. I would wonder, where would I take my children? Where would we escape to? I have no job, no home–where is home, anyway? I have lost my sense of home. It was a spiral out of control and away from everything we had ever known and so many little children looking to us and me for answers. It was such a sad and regrettable time.

CHAPTER SEVENTEEN

A FAMILY'S TALE OF WOE

We came to know anger, bitterness and separation. Every night the children and I would say goodnight to him, but he would never bother to walk up the two flights of stairs to tuck his children in, to read them a story or to check on their day.

I was angry and bitter; I was a single mother but I was sadder for my children having a father yet not. They were struggling in school, their father never once met with a counselor or teacher, or even with them to encourage or help them or understand their struggles.

I had to help each of them with their homework at night. I listened to their stories of broken friendships and broken hearts. I helped them find new friends and transported them when they found activities to join.

I helped them find new sports and transported them there, too. If I gave their daddy their schedule, he would certainly show up for their games, but he didn't show up to nurture them in the daily tasks of life or engage at all.

He only sought refuge in the basement when he came home from his job and he never quite engaged with our lives again. That is when the quilt unraveled. But how could I ever leave him? I just knew I must. How could I break my vow? How could I actually file a divorce?

But I knew I must. This was not healthy in any way. How would I find a way to financially provide for us? It was tough already trying to make ends meet for such a large family. When I would go to the grocery store and he would call us and say, "Don't buy sugar, don't buy chocolate chips. We don't need cookies or ice cream, don't spend extra. We just need spaghetti and sauce; that's all we need. Just buy the basics."

I knew that wasn't how I wanted to live. I wanted to give my children more, so I would use my credit cards to buy groceries. I needed gas, but he didn't care; he just put gas in his own car. He said I would have to find my own solutions. So, find my own solutions I would.

But, what would bring financial relief? Our credit cards were mounting, the pressures were mounting and the anger was constant. Nobody was pleased and nobody was emotionally healthy and peaceful. I decided then, I would pursue my MBA. A degree in business was sure to bring money and a constant job with a nice income; it was sure to bring a way out.

There was a lot of stress and constant threats. He didn't want me to pursue my degree because he knew that I would certainly leave him if I had that and he saw it as my ticket out; he knew that once I found good health again that I wouldn't need him and neither would our children.

Our life was full of chaos and yet there was both life and chaos in our home, we never stopped celebrating life in spite of the chaos. There was Boy Scout achievements, Eagle Scout awards, academic honors, field trips and baking cookies for the teacher, celebrating Christmas quietly, Easter dinners and plans every day to get through life.

But the everyday chaos often overshadowed it. Every two and a half minutes a volcano of anger would erupt. Every two and a half hours I would find a way to please the kids and engage them in an activity and I would distract them with a game in the other room.

I would go upstairs and tuck them into bed and then come downstairs to finish that argument that was still hanging in the air. I would corral him into the laundry room so they wouldn't have to hear us bicker while he was trying to drag them into the middle of our mincing words. We would be at the peak of our voices and there would be no resolution in site and I was praying for a way to diffuse the debate.

I knew that if I could get my degree I could come up with a solution that would minimize the heat. In the midst of all of the chaos, while he was at work, I would do my studies and my homework and look forward to the goal. When the kids would come home I would take care of their school projects, finish dinner and hurry to go take care of my exams online.

In the midst of him screaming at me, in the middle of him telling me to give up my degree and to "Pay attention to me!" and "Fix our marriage!" A marriage I knew I could never fix alone, for he had the power to change the things I could not, but the things that were deeply affecting each one of us.

I pursued my degree and I finished it in18 months. In spite of the chaos, I achieved yet another dream for myself. It wasn't because I needed a degree, but because I needed a solution for my family; a way to provide for the finances. During this time our dear friends, the Jakolas, the family who opened up their home to us to welcome us to Peachtree City, had a change of duty station and they family moved out of state ahead of the soldier this time. The soldier who had opened up his home to us was now our guest and it was nice to repay the gift of hospitality. He stayed behind to finish his tour of duty and he needed a place to stay; it was without thought he would stay with us.

When he stayed with us, of course he sat at our table for dinner, he was our house guest. But, my husband wouldn't like this. He would say, "Why are you cooking for him?" "Well, because he is a guest in our house, of course I would provide dinner and breakfast." My husband wasn't pleased with that unexpected token of hospitality.

And while he was free during the day and staying at the house, Bill, wanted to feel as if he were contributing to the house in return.

He asked, "Well, what can I do?" I thought about some of the things I wanted done at the house and I said, "You know, this light needs fixing and we would love to have these speakers installed outside so we can have music when we cook outside on the deck." He was happy to do it. While I was off volunteering in the kid's classroom, Bill was installing the speakers outside on the deck. My husband came home and encountered Bill installing speakers on the porch. I wasn't present, but I heard later that there was an argument and Mr. Arnold told Bill that he would have to leave our home. That it was his house and he wasn't welcomed to do repairs on his house while he stayed as our gues.

243

When I found this out I was outraged. "How could you not show hospitality to this man who had opened his home for seven weeks to us and all of our five children? How could you do that? You made him feel uncomfortable and unwelcome as our guest when he was trying to be generous and helpful. That is inhumane and something I simply can't tolerate. You have crossed the line for the last time." I was livid and embarrassed for our friends. So I told him, "Don't you dare come home."

And he stayed away for a week, sleeping in the pilot's lounge at work. I called to mend the fences with my friend who seemed to understand and forgive, but the friendship was never repaired after that. It was another loss I had to endure because of his irrational behaviors. I was too embarrassed to talk to my girlfriend after that. She tried so hard to help us but there was no solution, for the soldier was wounded

-permanently, so it seemed, and this was another defining moment for us. Despite me telling him to never come home, after a week he returned to the house.

How could I tell him to leave when there was nowhere else to go. There was no money, no credit card around, no answers; there was no more means to promote our separation. He had to be in the house. We managed to get through the fall and even Thanksgiving and it was soon Christmas time and another defining moment. The children were standing by the Christmas tree and I was taking pictures by the tree I didn't want to put up. My youngest daughter begged me to put up a tree for the holiday, so to make it easy, I bought a fresh cut tree from the local nursery. One roll of ribbon, which I created bows with, and one pack of ornaments would be the only decorations so I didn't have to unpack what we had stored away.

We decorated the tree and stood around it in our matching Christmas colored shirts and we took family pictures, which was tradition. I didn't want to be in the picture with him after all the confusion of the last year. I wanted to be in the picture with my children. My second son pleaded with me, "Please take a picture with us."

So to save face and to honor the moment for my kids, I agreed. I wanted to stand on one side with him on the other and the children in the middle, but my husband made a fuss, "Won't you stand by me?" he taunted. So of course, to make peace at this holiday time, I stood by him even though my anger was simmering. I stood by him putting on a face of sweetness for the camera.

But that didn't seem to appease him or anyone. He tried to argue that I should hold his hand and put my arm around him for the camera. He always wanted more than I wanted to give. I couldn't do it. My son just started crying -even at sixteen he just wanted to see us be amicable for one photo. "Can't you just do this for us? For Christmas–for this one picture. Can't you just ever get along?"

And he took off in a fit of emotion. We were able to snap one good family photo before all the confusion broke out. And that family picture will always symbolize the family at war to me; beneath the façade, trying to look picture perfect, was the brokenness of our family. The kids knew it, my son knew it and it broke my heart we couldn't just take one family photo for their sake. We were so broken, there was no more pretending. That was the last holiday we would celebrate together as a family.

CHAPTER EIGHTEEN

THE FOUNDATION FOR FAITH

Where would I turn when I needed help? My family was far away. My friendships were few as I had retreated into the demands of the house and my family. It would have to be my church. I returned to Holy Trinity, my parish, and found spiritual strength in the program Christ Renews His Parish, (CHRP).

A weekend gathering of thirty women coming together in sisterhood and Christ to praise Him, to wash away their wounds and their sadness, to look for comfort and encouragement and to share their stories.

It was a weekend retreat that would mark the beginning of my healing. Following the retreat, we would meet once a week for six months. In that time I was able to truly strengthen my faith and turn to this sisterhood of friends for encouragement, for clarity and for validation of my story. When I was there we would discern what our ministry would be; our gift to this six month process, for everyone in this group.

I knew that I had a story to share but it's not what I wanted to do for this new group of friends . I wanted to be in a position of leadership maybe to lead the group or as an event hostess to put on the next retreat, but I didn't really want to open up and witness .

But God would have it no other way, as we prayed and discerned it was quite clear that God had called me to witness. My challenge would be to witness before these lovely women who I could trust with my story and to write a story that would capture everything I had gone through without disclosing more than I was ready to. To witness to this group that they might find strength for their journey. (Learn more about my witness online at www.itsasweetlifegeorgia.com).

CHAPTER NINETEEN

FLEE BABYLON

F lee Babylon. It sounded like reasonable wisdom. I was in the middle of Babylon, a war field, a battle zone, a daily struggle for life, breath and peace. I prayed so many times, why could I not hear God's story, why could I not hear God's answers? This particular verse would not leave me, it haunted me; I turned to it over and over.

> *Leave Babylon, flee from the Babylonians!*
> *Announce with shouts of joy and proclaim it!*
> *Send it out to the ends of the Earth; say the*
> *Lord has redeemed his servant Jacob. They*
> *did not thirst when he led them through the*
> *desert, he made water flow for them from*

*the rock; he split the rock, and water gushed
out. There is no peace, says the Lord, for the
wicked.* -Isaiah 49:7

The Lord was telling me to leave Babylon? How could
that be? I think that the Lord wanted me to have peace,
indeed, but how ironic that I would get this exact scripture on our wedding anniversary, January 23, 2009. I
didn't want to believe that was the answer. I prayed it
over and over again. "Should I leave, Father? I see this
message but perhaps it's just me wanting an answer.
What is it you want for me?"

I found this message again on February 23, 2009–
exactly a month later? Certainly God would not tease
me with this scripture; surely I could not find it again
on my own on the same day, by coincidence. And then,
I saw it again as I prayed on April 23, 2009. Indeed, I
knew it was God punctuating this verse:

*Leave Babylon–flee Babylon. But announce
it with shouts of joy and proclaim it, for the
Lord has redeemed his servant.* -Isaiah 48:20

Was the Lord trying to give me freedom? He wanted
to ensure that I knew to trust Him, that I would not
thirst, that He would provide. God is so good to give me

encouragement in this time of confusion; if only I had the strength to listen. I began to pray, "Father, I know that when I leave and get out of the way, you can take care of your beloved son, Vincent, for he is your child and you care so much for him."

In this state, in our constant battle, in our engagement of power and control, there can be no victor; we weren't allowing God to take control. "Help me to leave and get out of the way so that you may bless us fully the way you intended. Please show me when, Father." And everywhere I looked there was a sign. There was a ladybug, a signal grace, constant confirmation.

One time we were in the Sprint telephone store and I was praying so earnestly in my heart and there was tension and angst filling the room as he completed a service transaction. "When, God, when?" I was earnestly imploring. And I turned around and there was a big, bold sign that said, "Now". Certainly, Father, certainly you do not speak to me through marketing advertisements. But, maybe so. Maybe God does speak to us with whatever is in our path that will reach us.

It was the strength I needed to know that the time had come. Now–indeed it was. As was true every time we came together, I pleaded with my husband. I tried to reason, to use logic and emotion; I tried to bring up things that were important to us. I tried to help him see

251

the vision of the goal of our family and the direction I wanted to go. I tried to show him how helpless I was to change things alone, how exhausted I was, how sick the environment was that we lived in every day and how it was affecting our children. I pleaded with everything I could muster. Evidently, I never used the right words. It always ended in anger and in a battle; we were entangled in both a battle of the wills and words. There was no way out.

I asked him one final time, so clearly, at the hockey rink as we arrived for yet another game for our son, "Please let's not do this, please go get help, please agree to change, please agree to do whatever it takes to save our family." But there was no reconciliation. He always ended it with, "If it's a divorce you want, fine. We'll get a divorce."

I was not asking for a divorce, I was asking for change—hope, freedom and for our relationship to exemplify the love he had committed to when we married. Nothing resolved that day and we continued to limp along.

Please don't let me mislead you by this walk of mine, personal to me. God does not condone divorce. God endorses marriage, healthy marriages that are covenants of love. God hates divorce. This is stated repeatedly in the Bible. Moses only advocated divorce in extreme situations or for stubborn hardened hearts.

But there was always a consequence. An exception is for marital unfaithfulness and remarriage only upon death of a spouse. I reasoned, my spouse was not faithful to the covenant of our marriage, he was emotionally and spiritually dead. I am certain, my heart had become stubborn and hardened at this point, too. The purpose of this book is something greater, to see the life and stress and sacrifices and cost of benefits to the military family. I know the battle belonged to God. As it says in 2 Chronicles: Do not be discouraged, the battle is not yours, but Gods. I will have to leave the judgment and the consequence in His hand. At that time, as I was surrendered to Him and seeking discernment, that scripture was repeatedly offered to me and with that, I found my peace and gave myself permission to leave.

Instead of reconciliation, what would come for us would be greater pressure, or perhaps, a doorway out–a job loss for him and more chaos for us. I would be sitting in my hairdresser's chair when he called me. He was quite emotional on the phone. "I just lost my job."

Oh no, we had become a casualty of the economy like so many others we knew of. So many people had lost their job and apparently, now it was our turn. We were already financially strapped, every credit card was maxed, we didn't know how we were going to pay our mortgage; we were struggling. We had no income and I couldn't seem to find a job. What were we going to do to provide for our family? I should have panicked, instead I prayed. Instead, I felt an immediate peace. I was immediately taken by a mild bit of emotion and the reality of the news, however, I was also very grateful, somewhat wondering what would be next because I knew this would lead to the solution we so needed, a solution we could never reach on our own.

It was three weeks later and we were at home in the kitchen and over heard him tell someone on the phone, "I didn't actually lose my job, they just kind of removed my position and they are keeping me in a holding pattern until they know what to do with me." You think he would have wanted to share that with his family; that we could have some peace and hope too.

That was a strange way to get the information. I was very frustrated and felt as if he had been deceptive. I was confused by the new information and angry for being misled. It was another time we would argue for a solution, but none would come.

It would be just three weeks later when he would have to leave to take the new job, now located in North Carolina. I knew for certain that I wouldn't be traveling with him. I knew for certain that this was the end. I couldn't leave our marriage on my own and he wouldn't leave when I asked him to. We couldn't separate on our own; no way could we come to a conclusion on our own.

He had a great work ethic and it was the only way he could provide for the family, so, I knew he would go, because he had no other choice. We went to a birthday party for his niece and his family had come to celebrate. It was uncomfortable and I could sense the tension was high; I knew our time was limited. There was no warmth left, just biding the time.

It was nice to celebrate the niece's birthday, but there would be sadness on the steps as we all said goodbye. He had already packed his car and as we left the birthday party he would leave and depart for his new job and we would return to Peachtree City to our home without him. It would be a period of strange and new transition.

I was grateful to have peace in the house. The children just accepted it as daddy got a job and he had to leave. They did not realize that he had left our family permanently and that we would become a new family unit. I think it was their form of denial, too. They knew it was coming and were glad to have the peace in the house, but didn't want to accept that their daddy would be gone as a result.

We didn't really talk about it, we just tried to accept it as if it had always been. It was hard because he left and never gave us his address. I guess he was just as happy to find his own way. In the first three months we saw him very little, maybe only on two occasions. We didn't know where he was living and we couldn't place him anywhere in our minds.

He left us only the automatic deposit of his retirement check which was only a small portion of our monthly needs, only about 20% of the funds that were flowing into the house. It was a ridiculously tough time and we had no groceries in the house which further pressed us to face the reality of his departure. A few friends came over and brought groceries with them because they saw my circumstance. There was no one for me to turn to?

During a time like this, you just have to buckle down and find your own answers. Nobody can come to your rescue or provide the answers for you. You have to dig deeper, think smarter and make it work. All the while we were nursing our wounds and I was helping the children through the transition.

Whenever he would call he would have some emotional garbage to feed to the kids. "Don't ever forget that I am your daddy, don't ever forget that I am the one who counts." It made the kids very upset. They were bewildered and felt torn by his conversations. "Are you never coming back?" they wondered. It was a very confusing time. And yet, it was five months later when I finally found his address by searching around online.

Five months without knowing where he had gone to live; it was an odd way to leave after 23 years of marriage. Knowing that we were desperate for food and gas money was also mean. I would ask him on the phone how I was suppose to take care of our kids and he said he didn't know what to tell me. He had no solution.

I guess he was in retreat mode himself, thinking that if he went to another state that we would be better without him and able to figure things out on our own. We were free from the daily chaos, but he was a warrior to the bitter end saying he would never give us a 'free place to live' and so I needed to find a way to support the kids and myself. Nine months after he left, I finally was able to confirm his residence and officially serve him papers.

I was working with a lawyer last year when I had first announced we were going to get a divorce, but after two months it didn't seem like a good fit and I had lost my nerve. We were still living in the same house together the first part of the year. While I was gathering my thoughts and my courage and trying to come up with a plan, his job loss forced the plan for us and he was soon plucked away to his new job in North Carolina.

Initially, I didn't know where I could even serve the papers and I was truly just trying to take care of our daily needs, our emotional needs, our financial needs;

the needs of managing a house. How would I move with twenty-five thousand pounds of household goods on my own, and where would we go?

I didn't want to fight through the divorce. I made it clear it wasn't about the money. It was about keeping my children and finding a way to start over. I soon learned and realized that the only advocate I had was myself and that I would have to create my own documents and find out on my own where he lived. Once I did, there were multiple obstacles and roadblocks with the delivery of the papers.

In fact, in the very first attempt, it went to the wrong person with the same name. It took us a couple months to actually identify where he lived and how I would officially serve the papers again. This frustration went on through the end of the year. Once he knew that I was serving papers, he started to come see the children twice a month.

They were happy to see him. They never really had a lot of free time with their daddy. I remembered in the beginning he would call me, "I don't know what to do with my time. I have them all day. Where should we go? What should we do? What restaurant should we eat at? How should I entertain them?" I gave my daughter advice to feed to him and in time, he seemed to figure it out.

I know that he had to shop for clothes for the youngest one and he didn't know what store she went to or what size of clothes she wore and he would call me and ask for advice. I fed it to him, frustrated but willingly, knowing that at the least, the children's needs were being met. He had been gone so often during their younger years, this was an opportunity for them to get to know one another and engage.

While he was deployed, he had a traditional view that the wife should take care of things, and I was a strong-willed leadership kind of gal, so I typically wanted to take care of things, anyway and this style worked. I guess he just set back and let me because he was tired from the battlefield. Who knows what reason he had to not fully engage, but this was his opportunity and he was going to have to learn by way of on-the-job training how to take care of and raise the children he was getting to know.

It was during a visit in October, a full year after I had announced that I was going to file for divorce, a full year after I had contacted my first divorce lawyer and had already had his papers served. We were at the ball field where he showed up for my daughter's game and in the parking lot we had another confrontation.

We had a discussion. "Jackie, is this what you want? Is this the life you want?" Of course it was not the life

I wanted it was just the choice I knew I had to make; the choice that had already been made for me. I never wanted a divorce and I didn't want to be the one to ask for it. However, if one of us didn't ask for it, we would certainly both bleed to death both and the children would come down with us.

He was like a Rottweiler who wouldn't let go of my neck until I was fully defeated. He was a warrior at battle and I felt like the victim. (Not that I am stating that I didn't contribute to the break down in any way. When things were bad, I could make it worse even when I was genuinely attempting to diffuse things). But, overall, I was the enemy he thought he was battling. And I no longer wanted to be the victim of his attacks. I wanted us both to find peace in our lives and I wanted our children to have the peace in life that they deserved.

I begged with him in the middle of that parking lot. I will never forget that October day, "Vincent, please, all I want you to see is that your children need you; that we are living an unhealthy life. That you are unhealthy, that you need help and that there are issues that have to be resolved. Please tell me that you can have an epiphany in your heart and that you just want to return to us with all of your heart and will do whatever it takes. I promise I will be there with you. I will help you through it. We will be a family together. I will forget everything that led up to this point and we will start again. But I need you to tell me that we will not live like this anymore."

And he stood his ground and said, "I am just a jackass, I will always be a jackass. You will just have to get used to it. This is the way I am and who I am."

I was blown away, even with that opportunity to fight for his family he instead chose his pride and ego. "How sad," I said knowing the time to throw down the towel had finally come. "Then that's a choice you make. I guess then if that's your answer, you choose never to be with your family again because we will not live like this any longer."

I left in tears, knowing that I had given him every opportunity to seek counseling, to seek help, to change and bring together the family I so desperately wanted to keep together, to come back and to heal us and to bring the loving father that we were so desperately missing in our family. This is all I really wanted for my children, but it was more than he could give.

He chose not to. He chose instead, to cling to his wounds from the battlefield; to cling the lies of who had become or who people said he was. All of which I knew was a lie. Though he clung to his anger and rage and fears and bullied to gain control when things were not, he was not a jackass; he was a good person when I met him, he had become hardened and hurt by what he had experienced in life and likely the frustrations of life in the military.

I know that God wanted to love him through the hurt and the pain, but he chose to cling to that pain instead of changing and doing the hard work that would be necessary to mend his family and let go of all that baggage. I knew in that moment, if he couldn't, I had to. I had to let go.

I had to flee Babylon. I knew I had to proclaim it with shouts of joy, and at least there would be freedom for me and my children and I prayed that God would eventually bring him freedom and peace, as well. As I signed every page of that divorce document in my lawyer's office, I prayed for my husband. With every signature that I put on every page, I prayed. "Bless him. Peace to him. May he be the father you have called him to be. Bless him. Peace to him..." I cried through the papers that I did not want to sign, but I knew it was the only way. I had to release him so that God could step in.

CHAPTER TWENTY

FAIRYTALE ENDINGS,
BUT NOT FOR US

Military spouses are not Army-issued, therefore there is very little leverage for the military spouse, especially once they become divorced. I was a military spouse without rules and without benefits. After dedicating my life, my love and my family to the Army, how would I end up without any military benefits?

I had also 'served' in the military for 16 years. My family had been impacted and we had sacrificed and struggled. I had supported him through every deployment and every military campaign, I had welcomed officer's wives, served in their community of morale welfare and recreation; I had led their community activities and nurtured many in the community.

But, now that the gavel had fallen, there would be no nurturing for me, no helping hand. It's the new 20/20/15 and 20/20/20 rule: You have to have been married at least 20 years, with 20 years of creditable service and the marriage and service must overlap by 15 years; respectively, you must be married 20 years of the 20 years of creditable service and all 20 years of marriage must overlap. We were married 23 years and he served 23 years of military service, so we passed the first two criteria, but only 16 years overlapped as service in the Army as a married couple, so none of the benefits were available to me, none of the service or sacrifice or deployments or nights without my spouse or spent raising a family of five alone were amended for. I lost my commissary privileges, my health insurance and my benefits. My service, though great, was no longer recognized. I was stripped of that after our divorce. I did qualify for the 20/20/15 rule which only extends one year of extended medical coverage, but as the paperwork was not clear or filed properly, I was to lose that privilege, as well, as my coverage dropped from Prime to Standard without my knowledge. It was brought to my attention two years post-divorce when my providers had refunded medical claims that insurance had originally paid and were now billing me for more than $2,000 in medical costs I incurred in that first transition year I should have had medical coverage.

There would be no access for me to medical care or military posts again. I had to turn in my military I.D. card, my favorite privilege, which I would use to get discounts at stores. Several stores honor the military and their families with 10% off and I would use it often to make purchases for myself or the children. I used to get discounts on hotels when I traveled. It was a nice privilege and a significant discount offered by the hotels. It really helped when the kids and I drove down to Florida to see my family and could break up the 11 hour trip with an overnight stay along the way. The discount made it fun. For me, my military i.d. was a badge of honor a symbol of my recognition for the service I offered–I had earned that military I.D. It was a sad day when I had to turn it in and it hit me like a rock.

Yes, these were tiny little losses I mourned, certainly nothing in the perspective of life, but things that had been a part of me for more than two decades of my life. I mourned the loss of my dream of being married happily ever after, I mourned the loss of never being married twenty five years and celebrating a silver wedding anniversary, the loss of not being the solution to my family's problem, not being able to fix things and give them the life they dreamed of.

I mourned the loss of failing, for generations, not being able to change the pattern of divorce, the loss of the prince that I thought would become my charming, the loss of what could have been: Our dreams, our hopes, to have a business, to have a home, to live happily ever after.

There would be none of that for me and the military would not support us. I would have to move a house that we had taken a lifetime to accumulate the contents of, I would have to move everything in it, physically and emotionally by myself. In spite of the fact that this move was indirectly a result of our military service and our retirement move, the military would not come and pack us up and move us this time. In fact, I would bear half the financial burden of the move, too, even though my income had been sacrificed at the hands of the military's demands. I would have to figure out how to assemble the pieces of this puzzle and bring hope to the children and create a new haven to call home.

I would have to help mend my children's broken hearts. I would be the one to help calm the anxiety. I would have to put my own broken heart aside and know that there would be no spouse waiting for me at the end of the day to help sort through the wreckage or to give sound advice. There would be no one but me to make sense of all of the confusion and the marriage that I had put so much hope and time into. I had to accept the fact that there was nothing I could do to control or change the situation.

Sadly, the military would not be there to support me. Not the JAG (legal) office, not the commissary, not the family team building support groups where I used to volunteer countless hours of my time. Nope. I would be on my own for this change of duty station. Because my husband was at Fort Bragg when he retired from the military and we had stayed behind in Virginia, I wasn't present for the retirement briefing and was told by my spouse, they waived my right for information. Even after 23 years of military service, I didn't even know where to begin or how to get services for myself as a separated military spouse or what I was still entitled to. I was going to have to soldier up on my own.

One day, I went to the nearest post and started knocking on doors, determined to find some answers. Everyone told me, "I'm sorry, it is a sad thing, but you have no more services. You have no medical benefits. You have no benefits and in fact, you have to turn in the I.D. Right there, on the spot, the military identification that I had earned legitimately from years of service and sacrifice, was confiscated. I used that card to buy groceries for my kids at the commissary, to buy my cosmetics at the exchange – my one benefit; I used the card to get discounts on shoes for the kids and hotels when we needed an overnight on the road and for discounted tickets when I took them to a movie or a theme park. In that moment, it was gone. I was disengaged from the military completely as if I had never served at all. My family was impacted equally because those tiny discounts sometimes made it possible for us to make the purchase or stretch enough to go to a movie. The hotel discount was the one I personally enjoyed the most. I appreciated the hotels like Marriott that recognized our contribution and provided special rates.

But, in that moment at the military counter, I knew I was powerless in more ways than one. I knew there was nothing I could do for myself but bootstrap it from here on out. Nothing I could do, but what my mother taught me to do as I watched her raise seven children on waitress coins night after night to provide for us, dig in for the journey ahead and turn to God for every good grace and provision.

I knew that only by the grace of God and sheer determination and persistence would I bring food to the table and provide for my family, to keep them clothed and engaged and provided for at school, to keep them fairly happy and free of anxiety, to help them make sense of all of the confusion we just lived through and were about to face, to heal the wounds, to semi-take care of myself and to make a way for us in the future to have hope and a home.

This was not exactly the fairytale we had dreamed of. We had gone from the land of castles and many opportunities, having traveled the world and living a life with lots of victories to the reality, the truth of this new definition of our family. The daily battle was over on the home front, but we still had plenty of battles in front of us. The war for us was far from over; there was smoke on the horizon. The enemy lines had been drawn and no truce flag was yet flying. We had endured many campaigns from Desert Storm to Operation Enduring Freedom. We had brought five children into this world and toured all of Europe. We had packed and moved nearly a dozen times. We had faced family deaths and financial crisis and storms one after another, but we couldn't overcome the battle wounds the military career had inflicted. It was time to retreat. There would be no victory cry for us; only whimpers of the wounded and sobs late into the night and a few more years wandering in the desert. But God is faithful and did not forget us and eventually, there was peace.

> *Praise be to the Lord, for He showed his won-*
> *derful love to me when I was in a besieged*
> *city.* -Psalm 31:21

Chapter Twenty-One

Out of the Ashes

W e lived in the same house until he moved for his new job mid-February 2010 and then the children and I remained in the house for another year until we moved December 2011. We didn't have the means to create separate households, so he came home twice a month to see the children and I would leave the house for the weekend. It was more stable for the children. They could still have a semi-normal life -see their friends, invite them over, have their own rooms, not have to schlep their belongings. I thought it was more peaceful, but in reality, it was likely more confusing for all of us.

Were we getting a divorce or not? Were we still a family, was there the possibility of reconciliation? Why does mom get to go have fun every weekend and we have to stay here? And the disparaging remarks the kids had to hear as their father's pain seeped out from choosing to stay in a home he knew was no longer his. I knew that had to end soon and when it was time to move from the house there would be no choice and we would have to make a clear, definable break; a boundary line in the sand.

Try as I might, no financial solution came – applications, networking – never availed to an open door. I spent time clearing out, hosting garage sales and generally carrying on with life. The kids responded with anxiety, bitterness and anger. Ironically, it was toward me instead of him. I was the one present. I was the one they could trust with their pain. And I wasn't the one providing any relief from the circumstances, no financial improvement – where were those promises of peace and joy?

Each one told me, "I understand. We couldn't live like that. I understand what happened." In fact, in days leading up to his departure, they would say, "Why does he have to be here? Why do we have to go home? Why do we have to live like this?" They would vent the way children do, fighting against the rage and confusion, but they so desperately wanted their daddy there. They truly wanted us to stay together as a family, but not under the conditions that were. They wanted the peace, the dream in their head and in their hearts of having their mommy and daddy in the same house.

When he left, it took him over a year to change his attitude toward the kids. He started showing up twice a month about ten months after the separation, slowly letting go of the family he once knew and getting to know the children for who they were, taking them out to eat and to the movies, something he never embraced while we were in the same house. At an earlier time, several years back, I asked him to take my oldest daughter to a movie when I couldn't because a last minute conflict.

He said, "Take my daughter to a movie? That would be strange. Daddies do not take their girls to the movies." And here he was, post-separation showing up as a Disney dad. Sometimes, He would take them to two or three movies in a weekend. He would take them to all of their favorite fast food restaurants and a nice meal in the evening; something I could no longer do because I was responsible for all the household bills and provisions and still no additional income. He would stay and play in the front yard and actually spending time with them and he was becoming the dad of their dreams.

So instead, they tried to make sense of the confusion by taking their pain out on me. They argued with me, they battled with me, they resisted the change and I had to keep it all together; keep hope and healing alive. Their anxiety came out in many ways as I managed the other great demands that come with a divorce.

During that time there were many prayers sent to Heaven and many prayers answered; prayers when I needed groceries, prayers when I needed gas in the car, prayers when I needed reprieve and prayers when I needed a friend. God heard me. God saw me. God was collecting all of the tears in a vial. For us, the family left behind, war still raged on.

This came up every weekend of visitation and every time he called. He would not let go of the fact that I was divorcing him. He hated the fact that he had lost the battle. He started calling the kids at unreasonable hours of the night, but at least he was calling them.

He would bring them mementos from his travels on his work trips; even though drawers overflowed with novelty t-shirts, he was at least thinking of them. He was winning their hearts as he was losing mine. During this time we were having a severe financial struggle and the divorce and the transition greatly added to the burden. He had been out of work for an extended period when we arrived, we had the replacement costs from our loss and I had not had a full-time paying job the entire time we had been there. Our financial demands had increased, our inflow decreased and our mountain of disaster left us with a mountain of debt, as well. There was no reasonable way to attack it.

There were many burdens on our plate and now our house would also become a casualty of this war as well as our household. We would have to say goodbye to the house we loved in spite of its burden; to the home that had welcomed our children when we were refugees from the hurricanes. We would lose many things: our hopes, our dreams, our house, our financial status, our future, my career, our marriage.

Some give all when they give their lives on the battlefield. Some sacrifice more than we know or have come close to experiencing. But our experience was pretty traumatic for us. My family had to learn to celebrate life and yet live in the chaos. My family had to realize there was glory with medals, honors and achievements, with promotions of rank, with tours of duty and places we loved, but we also had to have guts for the transition and to withstand the burdens and the pain of service.

We had to have guts for the deployments, guts for the endurance and guts for persevering. We had to give up many of our own dreams: being at one school, having lifelong friends, saying goodbye often to lives we embraced, being close to home, and being with grandparents and cousins as families should. We had to sacrifice houses of our dreams, cars of our dreams, toys and treasures and comforts of life because they would add to the household weight and take us beyond our limit. And when there was no financial provision for these things because military income has a ceiling and military spouses have difficulty in finding jobs to create additional income or have their hands full and limited time to make additional income, we had to make due. There was a life of benefits, but not without cost.

We received free hospital care and deliveries for each child's birth, we had great schools and caring teachers when we lived on military posts and we had a passport to travel the world, on rare occasion with free plane fare, if you weren't opposed to international flights in a jump seat and a flight without beverage service and pretzels. We had our household goods packed and shipped every time we had a new duty station. I got to enjoy being the mother of five beautiful children because we had an income we could depend on. They got to be raised in unique environments and still have a few unique memories to share. It was indeed, a life of benefits; but again, not without cost.

Some give all and this can't compare, but my family was also a casualty of war and we sacrificed everything we had from our dreams to our house, to our hope, to our future, to our marriage and to each other. We were left with battle scars and no one to nurse the wounds.

We were left alone to pick up the pieces. Military families truly suffer in a quiet and different way. It is who we are. We must be stoic for our soldier, for our families, for each other, but there is another side of the sacrifice. And we are human and sometimes we break. Military families are another casualty of war.

> *1 in 7 marriages formed prior to 9/11/2001 dissolve in divorce as a result of the stress of increasing deployments, according to RAND Corp, as cited by USA Today. 9/03/2013.*

This is a dismal statistic. America has the power and the opportunity to impact this sad truth.

Military soldiers and their families are carrying the burden of their brokenness. Hear their cries and resolve to take action. Stronger families make a stronger America.

CHAPTER TWENTY-TWO

HOW TO HELP AND CONNECT

The purpose of this book is to give perspective to what my family and I experienced so that you can have an inside view and an understanding of what a military family goes through in service to our country. I am hoping you will be deeply moved and motivated to reach out and help others who are still fighting for our freedom. I am hoping to see more American flags flying and less rants of taking the Pledge of Allegiance out of our schools. I am hoping Americans will wake up and embrace the country that we are and fight for what we have before it slips through our fingers. I am hoping you will immediately identify military families in your neighborhood and community and find a way to reach out or organize support for them through your community or determine to encourage a soldier overseas and find a way to ship off a care package today.

You simply need to do an internet search of military resources and you will find a wealth of information. The USO is always a good starting point as is Military.com.

A search of the Top Ten Books about Deployment for Military Families will also lead you to a reading resource list and provide good inspiration and information.

The Department of Defense (DoD), Community Relations maintains a list of resources. The American Red Cross Overseas, Fisher House and The Walter Reed Society are just a few of the larger umbrella organizations you can connect to for providing much needed support.

Freedom Calls Foundation, Operation Child Care and Operation Hero Miles are avenues to easily contribute. Donating frequent flyer miles through Operation Hero Miles could enable a spouse to go home for emergency reprieve or allow a spouse to accompany her soldier on leave post-deployment.

There are hundreds of ways to thank a soldier. Operation USO Care Package, Any Soldier, Operation Dear Abby and A Million Thanks are just a few organizations that assist with easy communications to soldiers.

Go the extra mile when you mail a package to a soldier and send a thank you note to the military spouse or children left waiting at home. This truly is the primary passion of my book, to take notice of the military spouses who sacrifice for our country, too. Yes, to note the children and the families and their burden. Yes, to support the soldier who makes the greatest sacrifice, but to notice the women holding up the soldier and the families in wait. My purpose is to bring you in to support the campaign so that we can stop thinking of it as a war 'over there,' a war on television, a war that is 'out of sight out of mind.'

There are ways to connect for the kids of deployed soldiers. Organizations are offering camps and scholarships and outings. There are quite a few books on the reading lists that could help a child as they have to wait for their parent to return from deployment. Sesame Street has created materials to educate and help children through deployment, as well.

These are great opportunities for the family to be supported. Maybe the spouse doesn't even have time to apply for the camp or to go look for the book and that is an opportunity for you to lend support whether you are a family member, a neighbor or a stranger – if you are an America, there is an opportunity for you to extend a helping hand. Helping others overcome obstacles is a great way to be of service.

Many great organizations are cropping up every day such as Wounded Warrior Project and Operation Home

Front. And even when you're playing your favorite sport you can be supporting the soldier who serves and can't be there playing alongside of you. Golf Tournaments to benefit soldiers such as Land of the Free and Birdies for the Brave are offered in many areas.

Don't limit yourself to big organizations and reaching soldiers overseas, my plea is for you to take notice of the military families at home. Make them dinner, send a note of encouragement, offer to drive them to church just for the company; buy them dinner, bring them bread, gather the neighbors to create a schedule of support, collect funds to fly in a mother or family member who can offer care for the children, make an appointment at a hair or nail salon. Simply show compassion. Support for our soldiers and their military service is more than a yellow ribbon, it is supporting and protecting the military families while they are deployed protecting us throughout the entire duration of the deployment, regardless of the length of deployment and the number of times they are sent away.

If you know of any veteran or family in duress or you encounter a situation you are not equipped to handle, please refer to a local chaplain, medical doctor or call the Veterans Crisis Line (800) 273-8255 or www.veteranscrisisline.net. This is the resource equipped to help, connecting families in crisis with Veteran Affairs Responders.

CHAPTER TWENTY-THREE

THE SPIRIT OF AMERICA RENEWED: A CALL TO ACTION

M ilitary families sacrifice so much with the soldier going away for periods of extended service. What would it be like if it was neighbor helping neighbor to ease the burden? What if we were to reach out when we know there is a military family going through this struggle when the soldier is deployed? Couldn't we show up to mow their grass once every week the soldier is deployed so the wife could have a little stress relieved or a little more time to write a letter to her soldier spouse? How about a babysitting voucher once a month or offer to take the car for a car wash and fill up or oil change? Couldn't we take out the garbage and bring it in for the family home without their soldier, and say, "Thank you for your family's service"? Because after all, it takes a strong family for a soldier to serve, it takes a village to support a family while their soldier is serving.

Couldn't we turn to the child whose father is fighting for our freedom and say, "Here is a gift card. Go take your mother for ice cream." Couldn't we reach out in ways that we have never thought of before?

Couldn't we become part of the war campaign by supporting those left home on the home front? Everyone has a role, not just the soldier on the battlefield. We have a duty to remember those serving and sacrificing us while we get to enjoy life as we choose. And support and care and encouragement should continue as long as the soldier is deployed, not just the first month and not just the month before they return. We need to come together as a community and keep the home fires burning every day they are serving; they serve every day for us. Families hurt and sacrifice and endure every day their soldier is gone.

We can also show support by hanging American flags on our doorposts. We can thank every soldier we see every time; simply a thank you or a hand shake. We can offer a $5 coffee card or pick up their check when we see them dining with their family or extend a restaurant gift card for them to treat their families. We can lend a hand to the families in wait by extending the same gratuity to the wives home managing children and chores alone. We can collect care packages every time we meet in book club and Bible study and send them overseas where soldiers are in need of encouragement and care. We can take a more active role of concern for the families in our very own neighborhoods being affected. Often times you will see someone mailing a package at the post office to an APO address – this is an indication they are encouraging a soldier–ask how you can help and get involved. If we would take care of the families at home, the soldiers could have more peace to focus on their mission.

If there was less stress on the family while they waited, perhaps we could help prevent marriages and families from cracking from the stress. The soldier would come back to a family refreshed and standing strong, to a place where they could come back to themselves refresh instead of fold under more pressure after unimaginable pressure.

What could we do to come together as a neighborhood, as a community and a nation? You will find more ideas on my website, www.*americadays.com.*

Spirit of America Days is a program I wrote following 9-11-2001 as a response to our nation's crisis. It is a call to patriotic action and volunteerism. It's a program I wrote as a response to the attacks on our nation and my platform for the Mrs. Virginia program. It is a program that calls us together to display our national pride, to celebrate our patriotic holidays between Memorial Day (end of May), and Fourth of July or (adapted) through Patriot's Day (9-11), and to come together as a community to volunteer, to help our military families, spruce up our neighborhoods and to help those in need. We spend many dollars and days on the traditional holiday season, why not one to love our country back to life? It is a vehicle for citizens to plug in to our communities and our nation and support our country as a patriotic America once again.

Our country is in need of a revival and a change of heart. People think our world is lost and it's too late to save the U.S.A., but it's not – there is still hope for our nation. God is patiently waiting for us to turn to Him for help. We must pray ceaselessly. We must restore our families, heal our hurts and help our communities – neighbor helping neighbor. Change is all around us, but it is so vital to the future of our nation that we come together and remember the founding principles and the core values that made us one great nation. Together we are stronger. United we stand. Spirit of America renewed in every community would create a new energy in our homes, our economy and our nation; there would be a new vibrancy and a new strength.

I look forward to the day when the spirit of America will be revived and renewed. We have an opportunity to today to plug in and do something; dust off the banners and let them wave. Won't you join me in this movement, to reignite our spirit? Won't you join me in the movement, to not only thank a soldier, but to also thank a spouse and support the military families who sacrifice so much? To nurture and comfort a family left suffering while their soldiers are deployed time and time again.

Won't you join me to fight for our freedom individually and to take a stand for America? This is our call to duty, America. This is our call to action, America. I challenge you to do something today. We can create a wave of compassion and offer a blanket of comfort for the military families left waiting and we can stand behind our military on so many fronts. This is not their war. This is *our* war. This is *our* freedom they are fighting for. This is *our* duty, too. This is our opportunity to serve our country. This is our call to action.

www.americadays.com

GOD BLESS AMERICA.

CHAPTER TWENTY-FOUR

LIFE MARCHES ON

Today, I am no longer living in the land of castles nor do I know anything more about military protocol, the state of the current community or the new battles they face. I no longer have the welcoming hand of the Army.

I can no longer go to the military post with my I.D. Post-divorce my i.d. card was confiscated, my privileges revoked. My children each have an I.D. card and when I take them to the airport gate, we can access the expedited military line, but I must go through the general line, no recognition of my 16 years of service, and wait. Then again it was a life of benefits I fully enjoyed but not without complaint and resistance and so maybe that is justice served and all I was owed. It just doesn't feel a just reward for dedicated service.

My children and I have found a new home that has brought us peace; there are flowers everywhere and the moving boxes are all gone. Their father shows up dependably and reliably every two weeks to see them. They have connected with him in a new way. My prayers have been answered. They have discovered their father and he has discovered them.

They have bonds that parents and children should have. They no longer have to struggle from the hardships and the sacrifices of being in a military family, they can finally just slip into life. Moves can come when we choose them to and dreams can be pursued without interruption. I am plugging in to the civilian community, as well. I have an army of friends, an army of wives, who know nothing of the military life I once knew, lifting me up to help me find my happily ever after in a new way. I wear my flag pin on Flag Day and I stand when the National Anthem is played whether on TV or in the stadiums. My boys proudly pursue these values in Boy Scouts and have earned the rank of Eagle Scouts. My girls walk in Fourth of July parades and show their patriotic pride, as well.

And as for me, my heart will always stay true to the land I love, the country my entire family each sacrificed

THE MILITARY FAMILY: A CASUALTY OF WAR

for. A house divided cannot stand – my marriage is an example of that, but a nation united will prosper.

God will prove to the world that He is God by doing the impossible -causing warriors to set their captives free. As I have personally experienced, God is faithful to fulfill His promises. Sometimes, this means doing the impossible to make them happen, but nothing is too difficult for our Amazing God. When I could not find a route to freedom, God helped me find my way. God promises Restoration of Israel and He promises restoration for me, too. The days of battle are behind me and the days of hope and a brighter future are before me.

Yes, captives will be taken from warriors, and plunder retrieved from the fierce; I will contend with those who contend with you, and your children I will save. -Isaiah 49:25

MAY GOD BLESS AMERICA

ABOUT THE AUTHOR

J acqueline Marie Atkinson Arnold was born in Miami, Florida and simply considers herself a southerner, having lived in many states in the South. A former military spouse of 23 years, she enjoys volunteerism and giving a voice to the military spouse and family. She is a mother of five, an author, a key note speaker and principal of It's a Sweet Life Georgia.

She holds two masters degrees, the former titles of Mrs. Virginia, 2003 and Top Ten, Mrs. International and serves as an Ambassador for Christ. She is the published author of ***Eat, Love, Praise Him,*** a God-inspired four-part series of one woman's personal journey of faith. She has been to more than 30 countries and pursues travel, photography, golf and helping others believe in their dreams as her personal passions.

Eat, Love, Praise Him!
While enduring a decade of life's storms, she learned to dance in the rain, live on His grace and praise His holy

name! There are stories of disaster, divorce, hurricanes and happiness, love and heartbreak, travels and culinary delights. Together, the series unravels this resilient woman's life and reveals a rags to riches, riches to rags to redemption and happily ever after ending with dreams come true. She is a prophetic writer whose stories are based on her personal journey of faith and God's provision of modern day miracles.

Eat, Love, Praise Him! Series
Book One: **E**at, **L**ove, **P**raise **H**im! Unpacking Your Dreams on a Journey of Faith
Book Two: e**L**ph – A **Love** Worth Fighting For (Based on a True Ruth and Boaz Love Story)
Book Three: Eat, Love*, Praise Him!* Finding Boaz – Becoming the Treasured Bride of Christ

Coming Soon:
Book Four: ***EAT!*** *Love, Praise Him! Travel Journals of a Dream Believer (A Story of Redemption)*

Released September 11, 2014: The Military Family: A Casualty of War *As Told By a Former Military Spouse*

To learn more about this patriotic program supporting volunteerism and patriotism visit: www.americadays.com

To learn more about Eat, Love, Praise Him! or to book Jacqueline as a speaker at your next event, contact her at: www.itsasweetlifegeorgia.com

CPSIA information can be obtained at www.ICGtesting.com
Printed in the USA
LVOW04s0751310814

401703LV00004B/9/P